EMOTIONALLY
wounded
SPIRITUALLY
strong

TARRAN CARTER

EMOTIONALLY wounded SPIRITUALLY strong

VICTIM NO MORE—SEVEN HEALING PERSCRIPTIONS

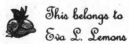
This belongs to
Eva L. Lemons

TATE PUBLISHING & Enterprises

Published by Tate Publishing & Enterprises, LLC
127 E. Trade Center Terrace | Mustang, Oklahoma 73064 USA
1.888.361.9473 | www.tatepublishing.com

Tate Publishing is committed to excellence in the publishing industry. The company reflects the philosophy established by the founders, based on Psalm 68:11,
"The Lord gave the word and great was the company of those who published it."

Book design copyright © 2011 by Tate Publishing, LLC. All rights reserved.
Cover design by Scott Parrish
Interior design by Stefanie Rooney

Published in the United States of America

ISBN: 978-1-61663-448-3
Body, Mind & Spirit, Healing, Prayer & Spiritual
11.01.27

ACKNOWLEDGMENT

This book is dedicated to my loving mom, a mother who has taught me since I was a little girl, "Do unto others as you would have them do unto you." Mom, thank you for teaching me such qualities of life. If I ever needed an example of faith, you have been a valiant example. You have always given to others, in spite of your own pain. In distress, you took courage to protect your daughters by standing up to the enemy and walking away from the only life you knew. Your tenacity to overcome the many obstacles of life has enabled me to view life optimistically. God has allowed me to come through your loins, just so you could see that God can take what the enemy meant for evil and turn it into a beautiful rose. He is the God who is able to raise up a daughter that was destined for destruction and change the enemies' prognosis by redeeming and delivering her. Mom, victory has already been decreed; it has already been established. It is awesome that we can smile and rejoice together in jubilation.

I love every one of my sisters. To each of you, thank you for being my sister. Siblings don't get to choose each other. Many times, you just have to accept what you have. You all are unique and wonderfully made, and I thank God for each unique personality. God has promised us lives of wealth and posterity, salvation, and eternal life. Therefore, we will continue to serve the only wise God. The curse is broken, and God is doing great things. Hallelujah!

To my husband, you are the joy of my life, and I could not have written this book without you. As I wrote from the tablets of my heart, I was reminded of the many times you stood by me and walked me through the healing process. Since we accepted the Lord as our savior, our life has never been the same. It has been uphill—from victim to victory. Everything has changed for the best, and we are in the right place to be blessed. Thank you, honey. You are truly a man of God: loving, patient, and humble. You are the best lover, father, and friend—truly a lover for life.

To my daughters, I get to watch you bloom into beautiful roses, and as you are blooming, God is still perfecting that which concerns you. Thank you for all of your support. You are the daughters that any mom could ask for. I sometimes miss the days of preschool and nursery rhyme books. God lends us our children for a time, and he trusts parents to raise them in the way that they should go, which is the way of the Lord. Again, as I mentioned with my siblings, we don't get to choose with whom God entrusts us, but we do have the responsibility to handle them with loving care. Well, ladies, God gave me lovely girls with unique personalities, and I thank him for that. I trust and thank God each day for your salvation.

I also thank each one of my spiritual daughters

and sons of Perfecting Praise Ministries. You each have come to the ministry with awesome gifts that make the ministry what it is today. Thank you for supporting me in my efforts to write this book, and I hold your support dear to me.

Last, but not least, I dedicate this book to my oldest sister Joanna, who was a victim of rape and recently has gone on to be with the Lord. I will never forget how Joanna never complained of her pain through her battle with cancer. I will never forget how she never chose sides with her sisters. She was the matriarch, the oldest sister—a woman of strength. Because she has always been there for me as a big sister, it would be remiss if I did not honor her and show my appreciation for all of her support. Many days, while writing this book I sat with her at her bedside in the hospital. Even in pain, Joanna never thought about herself. She would look over and give words of encouragement to me while insisting that I complete this project. As I reflect back, I hold back the tears for she will be forever missed.

TABLE OF CONTENTS

SPIRITUALLY
strong

TO THE READER

Emotionally Wounded is a book for the spiritually wounded—those who have suffered from child abuse, incest, molestation, and rape. Each chapter reveals a deeper dimension of the power of God and demonstrates your authority to overcome the enemy. The book walks you through the deliverance process, as your spirit accepts that you are victorious. As you read the healing prescriptions, the healing process will begin. You will also gain a better understanding of why it was *you* who was sought out by the enemy.

God has released me to write about what has been locked up inside of me for years so that deliverance, restoration, and joy will come to many. I want to take you back to the little child; this is where most of us have to journey back to in order for deliverance to occur. Though painful, if you have not healed appropriately, then you are still infected. I was tired of living in uncertainty, pain, and wretchedness. I needed God to do something, and He did.

Unquestionably, my story is one of many stories that have been told concerning molestation. I am not a clinician or psychologist; I am a pastor who suffered the effects of molestation for several years. I have been authorized and equipped by God to write about the abuse and its diabolical affects and effects.

Like Paul, an author in the New Testament, I am also a bondservant of Jesus Christ. I don't write to update Jesus—Jesus cannot be updated. Nor do I write to bring a new revelation of Christ, Jesus said everything that needed to be said. I simply write what I know, for the household of faith, that you would be enlightened by my experiences and healed by the power of His Word.

Unconditionally, I want to help you understand the enemy's kingdom strategy. Though Satan has an organized kingdom, you can be equipped to hit the bull's-eye every time you pray for your family and yourself. You can be restored back to your natural state. Not only was I ambushed, but my family—my mother and six sisters—were ambushed. We never saw the enemy's attack.

I never knew that victory, God's topical plan, awaited me. It is an existing plan, established from the beginning of time, yet it is also a contemporary plan, uniquely designed to bring me into who I am today. I was ambushed from within until I realized who created me—Jesus Christ. Tears of joy have filled my eyes and graced my cheeks in the knowledge that God's grace and mercy have made a way for the enemy's plot to fail, thereby saving me from destruction.

Paul writes in the New Testament, "We are hedged in on every side but not cramped *or* crushed; we suffer embarrassments *and* are perplexed *and* unable to find a way out, but not driven in despair; We are pursued, but not deserted; we are struck down to the ground, but never struck out *and* destroyed" (2 Corinthians, AMP).

God is a redeemer, restorer, and the lifter of your head. He does heal and His will is that we not perish from sickness, pain, wickedness or sorrow. Hallelujah!

Please allow me to be real and talk about real issues concerning the subject matter of this book. I want to touch on conditions and spirits that the enemy would like to keep hidden so that he can posses, control, and even hide within his victims, thereby prohibiting deliverance.

God is the greatest counselor ever known. Oh, you may have gone to many clinicians and psychologists. Yes, they are professionals in their fields, so I take nothing away from them, especially those who have godly principals and seek the guidance of the Lord for their own guidance. Nevertheless, God Jehovah Rophe is our healer.

It is important that we pray the "prayer of agreement" before you start reading this book. Satan will try to make you tired and disinterested. He knows that your blessings and deliverance will be manifested in the completion of this book, and that your life will never be the same. The book of Matthew 18:19 (AMP) in the New Testament records, "Again I tell you, if two of you on earth agree (harmonize together, make a symphony together) about whatever [anything and everything] they may ask, it will come to pass and be done for them by My Father in heaven." Therefore, I agree with you that as we pray, our prayers are released into the atmosphere and perform our request. There will be a response from heaven, because God does hear our prayers and grant petitions. After we pray, expect God to move; watch the manifestation of change in your life. Do not be surprised. Just praise God, because it is going to happen. Know that it is too late to turn back or put the book down; you must move forward. Victory awaits you.

Pray this aloud using your God-given authority. Call your name out in the blank spaces.

Father, in the name of Jesus, I, _____ thank you for your goodness and mercy toward me. You are my healer and my deliverer—the maker of this universe. You sit on the circle of the earth, and my face is in the palm of your hand. I repent and ask for forgiveness from every sin that is known and unknown to me. Nothing prevents me from reaching the heavenly places in Christ Jesus. In Psalms 40:7 David writes "I, Lo, I come in the volume of the book that is written of me—to do the will of my Father." I am confident of the power and authority that my God has invested in me from the beginning of time. Therefore, I bind every diabolical assignment and attack of the enemy that is purposed for me, and I return them to dry places. I command the enemy to loose his hold—my mind is free to comprehend—apprehend all that I read in this book. I declare that the spirit of heaviness and sleepiness cannot and will not overtake my conscious and unconscious state while I am reading this book. Whatsoever is bound on earth is bound in heaven; whatsoever is loosed on earth is loosed heaven. I, _____, decree today that I am alert. For where the Spirit of the Lord is, there is liberty. No weapon—intrinsic or extrinsic—formed against me shall prosper.

Draw me close to you, Lord, that I may hear your voice. The Word of the Lord says, "My sheep know my voice." As I read the scriptures, I decree that I am the recipient of illumination and being the beneficiary, through Christ, I obtain revelation—communication and relationship with God. Revolutionize my thinking so that my life will never be the same. Lord, let me see your perspective concerning life issues and concerns. I trust you to direct my footsteps that I am not moved by my own or by man's intellect, for that will only separate me from you. I decree that while I am reading this book, the child in me will be healed.

Give me your wisdom and understanding. I am like Solomon; I don't have enough, and I don't know enough unless you show me. Lord, cover me in the blood of Jesus. Where the blood of Jesus is applied, the enemy cannot enter.

Today, I look to heaven as Jesus did and declare that I am healed by the power of God. Though my senses may not recognize the healing, without a doubt I know that the manifestation has already begun. I am victorious. I am gaining new ground today, and as I read each page, I gain new heights in God. I am the head and not the tail. I am the first and not the last. The Lord has prepared a table for me in the presence of my enemies. I am made in my Father's image; therefore, I have his DNA. I am his beloved child, and there is nothing the enemy can do about it.

This prayer is already settled in the heavenly realm, and I, _____, settle this prayer in the earthly realm. In Jesus' name, Hallelujah!

TO THE ONCE VICTIM

While reading this book, you will come to realize you are no longer the victim, but the victor. God wants to build up what was once torn down—that self-esteem, wholeness, and confidence would return unto you— indubiously enabling you. A transformation will begin to take place and you will never see yourself in the same light. Today, you are in the best place to be blessed. You are no longer the outcast.

The scripture tells us, "The Lord doth build up Jerusalem; he gathered together the outcast of Israel" (Psalms 147:2, KJV).

"For I will set mine eyes upon them for good, and I will bring them again to this land: and I will build them, and not pull *them* down; and I will plant them, and not pluck *them* up" (Jeremiah 24:6, KJV).

God desires to build you up; He desires to heal and deliver. God erases the shame and replaces it with His glory. You are stronger than you think. I speak from experience and I understand the plight of the abused. My experience has authorized me, this forum, to advise that you are no longer the victim but victor.

THE AMBUSH

I am now an adult with a family of my own, living in my own home, but this took place at the house where I grew up—a house that my parents sold years ago. I have not been in this house since some of my sisters were adolescents, and I was in college. I have had many dreams of the house, and I vividly remember each room—the colored wallpaper; the blue linoleum floor; the sky blue vinyl seat cushions; and the white, catty-cornered, custom-built glass-front kitchen cupboard.

The dream begins with me in the den, which was in the basement. It was approximately 11:00 p.m., and I was making my way to the white door that led to the pantry. I placed my hand on the doorknob and turned the knob to open the door. I walked past the white washer and dryer; everything was still in its place. I passed the table we used for homework, board games, and folding clothes. Then, while passing the old wooden workbench, where the tools were so organized on the wall, I remembered my father using many of these tools—vice grip, saw, etc. Some of these tools, I had also learned to use. The images were so clear.

As I slowly walked toward the pantry and cedar closet, I saw my sister, Loretta. She was born after me, and we were close in age.

Loretta and I both knew something was wrong. We were under attack, and our adrenaline started pumping. We needed to make an escape, and the window just above our heads was our only way out. Loretta pulled the ladder down to reach the window. *Red flag,* we both noted.

We were just below the window, and the light was shining bright. We were in view of whoever was in pursuit of us. Quickly, Loretta reached up to pull the long, white string that hung from the oval light bulb. When she pulled the string, the light mystifyingly turned from a bright white to a dim red. We could only see our silhouettes. Loretta climbed up a couple of steps on the ladder and reached for the window. She grabbed the latch and pulled the glass pane open, which left the window screen still in place. We looked out of the window. Though it was dark, we could see a male figure bent over with his face pressed to the screen.

He asked, "Where can I find Maple Avenue?" Immediately, I backed up. My forehead and eyebrows crinkled as I drew my head back. I knew without a doubt something was wrong. All of my senses were heightened as though I had gulped down a pot of espresso.

Why would a stranger be at our basement window with his face pressed against the screen, asking a question about a street? I thought. *This is not cool.*

While my mind was trying to sort things out, I heard a creaking sound. It was the floor above us. I looked up at the old ceiling, with its wooden beams and pipes, and I knew it was coming from the kitchen upstairs. I left my sister and went through the door, and slowly, with my back pressed against the wall, both hands holding the rail—I walked up the stairs toward the kitchen. I scanned the kitchen from the open doorway—there he was. I grabbed him, and after tussling for a minute, I had him in a headlock and was ready to snap his neck.

It is not clear where or how I obtained it, but I had a broomstick in my hand. With much pressure and strength, I pressed the broomstick against his throat. He gasped for air, and before I snapped his neck, he said, "And you never knew what I was."

I proceeded to press the stick against his neck. His neck snapped, and he dropped to the floor. "Loretta!" I yelled. I took off down the stairs, missing a couple and jumping past the rest, to the den floor. I ran through the door, around to the pantry to find her. She was still on the ladder, slumped over, with an unusual ring around a large bullet hole in her throat.

"A sniper—I never heard the attack! How many are there?" I yelled. I ran up the stairs, through the kitchen, into the living room, and toward my parents' old bedroom. I looked toward the hallway. My eyes honed in on an image. I didn't know if he was real or a figment of my imagination. He had the appearance of a man—tall and fit. He looked as though he had come out of a jungle, but I knew this was not a scene in a cartoon or comic book. He was dressed with nothing but a leaf-like skirt from waist to knees. He was one of the snipers, and he was exposed and in motion for his next victim. This hideous character knew I saw him, and he stopped. He turned his head to look at me. Robotically, he turned his head back toward his target and proceeded toward my sister's room.

He didn't come after me! I thought. Quickly, I went into my parents' room, but my mom was gone. Though I never saw her, I knew it was too late.

What do I do now? I thought. *Should I go through the window?*

I was running out of options. Instantly, I heard the voice of the Lord say, "Do not go through the window." I stopped and looked at the closet to see if I could hide—I didn't have a plan of attack. In the midst of this confusion and uncertainty, I stopped. I needed a strategy to move forward … then, I woke up.

This was a dream. The snipers symbolize a demonic force—agents in mission to destroy each family member. The sniper spoke directly to me. He wanted me to know that while he and his cohorts were in position to destroy the fabric of my family, we never knew who or what they were. The dream is a depiction of the abuse that happened to my sisters and me when we were little girls. Nevertheless, Satan has been unveiled. He is exposed, and he knows that I know who he is. It was an ambush—a sneak attack. Snipers were on the scene to destroy the plan of God for my family. They were in pursuit to cause injury and cut off the breath of God, leaving us lifeless to this world. This dream revealed the plan of attack. Without a doubt, it is significant that God, the greatest strategist ever known, wanted me to wait for his God-given strategy and I have. God spoke to me through this dream and said he had governed my plan of action, which also provoked me to write this book. God has a plan and knows the way that we should take. If we would allow him to be God and Lord in every aspect of our lives, we would avoid so many mistakes.

To ambush someone is to have an organized plan of attack. The prey is generally oblivious and vulnerable, and the main objective is to destroy. The ambusher is hidden for the purpose of successfully carrying out the mission. Many children and adolescents who were ambushed never fully understood the devices of the enemy, and because they were in the childhood stages of helplessness and dependency, they had no other choice but to submit to the powers that be. If the enemy can disrupt your life at the developmental stage, he can change the trajectory of your life. His mission is to create his destiny for your life—a life that would tie you to his life support until he snatches the cord, which he will do if you are not delivered.

To understand his objective, you must understand what life support is. A person who is in need of life support has generally suffered serious traumatic injuries from something such as a car accident, a debilitating stroke, heart attack, or any number of vital organ failures. Some examples of life support include mechanical respiration, heart and lung bypass instruments, defibrillation equipment, and renal dialysis. In most cases, a person who requires life support is unconscious.

Rape, incest, child abuse, and molestation are traumatic experiences. Satan's insidious plan is spiritual and physical death. The plot is to disturb and interrupt the innocent nature of God by shocking a person's spiritual being, thereby, hooking them up to his life support. Satan's tubes run into their hearts and lungs, leaving them in a comatose state. He then slowly suffocates the plan of God from their lives. Consequently, they cannot hear or see God, and often they hate God. John 10:10 (KJV) demonstrates this, "The thief cometh not, but for to steal, and to kill, and to destroy…"

Satan is camouflaged—masked to hide the predator spirit—so you cannot detect his presence or plan. He is cunning and able to beguile the senses of his prey. His covert scheme enables him to live and function among family and friends and not be detected. The affects of his ambush leave his victims impaired psychologically and emotionally—the effects are long-term.

Let's go a little deeper to understand his plan. It

was decreed before we were born. Satan knows his final destination. Therefore, he has commissioned himself to violate, disrupt and destroy as many people and families as he can, by any means necessary. The goal is that man would sin—miss the mark and like Satan, be destined for the lower regions of this world. As we read earlier, he is after the seed to destroy the family legacy. Revelation 12:7–8 tells us, "Then war broke out in heaven; Michael and his angels went forth to battle with the dragon, and the dragon and his angels fought. But they were defeated, and there was no room found for them in heaven any longer. The huge dragon was cast down *and* out—that age-old serpent, who is called the Devil and Satan, he who is the seducer (deceiver)of all humanity the world over; he was forced out *and* down to earth, and his angels were flung out along with him" (AMP).

After the battle of Lucifer—now Satan—and his angels, Satan was convicted, judged, and the decision of execution was made. God does not relent; he cannot return. There is no room in heaven for him any longer.

Unquestionably, he knows his destination—the lower region of the world and eternal fire.

Understand that Satan was full of fury when he was flung from heaven. Full of wrath, knowing he had only a short time, and because he felt there was nothing to lose, he devised a plan to ambush the woman. Satan is after the seed. Though Satan's claim is the male seed, in the process of attaining it, he must go after the only being who can house the seed, and that is the woman. In the process of going after the male, every seed is attacked to ensure the plan is carried out.

Revelation 12:13 states, "And when the dragon saw that he was cast down to the earth, he went in pursuit of the woman who had given birth to the male Child" (AMP).

The dragon here had already been defeated and was relentless in retaliatory efforts, struggling to retain claim on the planet he lost. He was in pursuit of the woman, the witnessing church, and the hope of glory. If he could have killed the woman's spirit before conception, there would have been a chance of stillbirth or some type of deformity at birth. Satan knew that the woman was special to God, that God purposed and entrusted her to incubate and nourish the seed in order to bring forth the king, Jesus Christ and because of The Lord's divine decree and purpose, there was no chance of Satan's plan coming into fruition.

Why Me?

Many have asked, "Why me?" Let's answer that question. Well, why *not* you? Author and Pastor Maurice Johnson wrote, "Destiny is the predetermined purpose of being that lies in you." You were sought after before birth.

Before you were born, God knew you. Before you were imagined or conceived, God formed you. You were predestined before the foundations of this world. Your name had life before you were conceived. To prove this, remember Isaiah, Ezekiel, Joel, and some of the other prophets, who spoke about Jesus before he was conceived of his mother Mary. Let's go to the Word of God to demonstrate this:

- "A virgin shall conceive" (Isaiah 7:14; Matthew 1:23 - KJV)
- "A Child is born. A Son is given" (Isaiah 9:6; Luke 2:7–14 - KJV)

Isaiah and some of the other prophets did not imagine these things on their own; they were inspired by God to write them. God revealed these things and anointed them to write them down. This proves the Messiah's name was living in this world before his conception. How awesome is that? Before your parents could conceptualize who you were or would be, God knew you. God himself uniquely and wonderfully made you in the image of him.

Submission to God allows him to order our footsteps. If we are his sons and daughters, then we have our Father's DNA. God is the only god who can create man from the red clay and dust of the earth, and produce such excellence as you and me, and Satan knows this. Therefore, we don't belong to Satan. Actually, we are not our own, for we have been bought with a price—Jesus Christ paid the price for you and me.

From the beginning of time, Satan's great commission was to separate man from God—to curse the relationship so that man would be driven out of

God's presence and we would not receive the fullness of joy. When we are driven from our natural surroundings, we scurry and wander to find our places in life, when God has already given us abundant life. We fight to get what God has already given us. Eve allowed the enemy to convince her to give up what God had given her—abundant life. I wrote a poem that deals with this topic.

Unfamiliar Territory

Wounded and left for dead, we are like
children walking on unfamiliar streets.

We are lost. In one hand, we hold tightly
an old blanket—our past—while with the other
hand, we suck on our fingers—our security.

From time to time, tears of oppression
and distress stream down our cheeks as
we look up to strangers for help.

For immediate assistance, we flag
our wet fingers in the wind.

We are looking for love, security, and direction
in anyone who looks like they can help.

Only strangers and people who
don't care are attracted to us.

The detection has been made—we are wounded.

Regardless of past or present circumstances, we can have the fullness of joy and walk in the path of life, which we will learn how to do in the following chapters.

"Thou will show me the path of life: in thy presence *is* fullness of joy; at thy right hand *there are* pleasures for evermore" (Psalms 16:11, KJV).

When we desire to know the things of God, we become acquainted with the knowledge of God and can discern and perceive the things of God. Hence, darkness cannot perceive light. Darkness does not understand the things of God, but if we are in light—in the presence of God—God shows us the way and passing of life. When we allow God to guide us, he is in front of us and before us; he is our sight and countenance, and we are open to his will. We have fullness, satiety, and abundance. Our voices are joyful, our cries are joyful, and our banquets are joyful. In the direction of our Lord, there are perpetual pleasures forever.

Let's answer the question, "Why you?" Satan does not want you to receive all that God has for you. There are blessings with your name on it and they were preordained for you before the foundations of this world. If Satan can get you to believe a lie—no hope—no joy, he can separate you from the will of God. Satan knows when you are separated from the Father; there is no power, and you are vulnerable to his tactics and devices. Polar bear cubs cannot see when they are born. The mother bear keeps them in the den to protect them. For approximately two years, the mother bear protects and teaches them how to hunt for food. It is a mother's—human or any other creature's—instinct to protect her babies once they are born or hatched. Left alone, they are vulnerable to and prey for the enemy.

Password for the Healing Prescription

Before we move forward, let us talk about salvation. Have you given your life to Christ? If you have—great—you are covered, and you have the password. If you are not saved, why not take this opportunity to give your life to Jesus. Repent of your sins. Give the Lord your sins, your worries, and your past. Now that you believe, he is of the Father who sent him. Ask the Lord to be Lord over your life, allowing him to become your present and your future. Once you've given your life to Jesus Christ, ask him to fill you with the Holy Spirit.

Acts 19:2 asked, "Have ye received the Holy Ghost since ye believed?" (KJV) Because you believe, and there is no doubt in your heart, the Lord will fill you with the baptism of the Holy Spirit—the evidence of speaking in tongues. Hallelujah!

The angels in heaven are now rejoicing. You now have the password—*Jesus*. You can now fill the prescription I will prescribe, and it is free. The password allows free access to his antidote. It is the cure and his every promise. I guarantee you—your life will never be the same. With salvation is the full package of healing, wholeness, peace, joy, and a life full of prosperity and wealth. The gamut; is what Jesus offers.

Training Ground

The first thing I need to establish is whether you have ever been trained for battle. If not, don't get in the ring just yet. The devil will set up a full-fledged attack by assaulting your finances, your health, your family, and your faith. This is called the backlash. We have a powerful weapon, and that is the Word of God.

Don't worry. The first strategy is a launch attack. We are going to unleash the powerful Word of God on the enemy. While Satan is in the ring, waiting for us to enter, we are going to sling the Word of God—as David did to Goliath—into the ring. The Word of God will hit, penetrate, and destroy the works of the enemy. In the interim, we will pull down strongholds, and because we are covered in the blood of Jesus, the counterattack of Satan fails every time.

The Apostle John writes in the New Testament, "Because greater is he that is in you, than he that is in the world" (1 John 4:4, KJV).

The Amplified Bible says it like this: "Little children, you are of God [you belong to Him] and have [already] defeated *and* overcome them [the agents of the antichrist], because He Who lives in you is greater (mightier) than he who is in the world."

My sister, my brother—it is a fixed fight. Because God is the greatest strategist ever known, he will give us the strategies. Professional strategists and coaches, with all of their degrees, have nothing on God.

The Lord prepares and takes us through the processes of life. This is our training ground. Even though we may desire to skip this step, it is necessary for preparation. The wise and simple of this world cannot understand God's methodologies. As always, the devil has no clue of God's plan in your life. David was a great warrior; his training ground was among the bears and lions. The strength and weight of the bears and lions propelled David from one level to the next and prepared him to defeat Goliath with one smooth stone. His combination of faith, the Word of God, and his own strategic armor enabled him to hit the target with accuracy and bring the uncircumcised Philistine down.

According to 1 Samuel 17, the Philistine presented himself for forty days, morning and evening, defying the armies of the Lord. The number forty represents a generation and time of testing. The armies of Israel were in distress because they feared the giant. It took someone from another generation—David, the youngest son of Jesse—to stand up to the test.

Goliath was a self-absorbed bully who challenged those who feared him as well as anyone who was not afraid. He declared that whoever took him up on the challenge would be defeated, and their flesh would be given to the fowls of the air and the beasts of the field.

This is what Satan has declared on us, but we must be like David and superimpose the Word of God over the declarations of the enemy. David accepted Goliath's challenge without fear. First, he set the record straight by letting Goliath know who he really was—an uncircumcised Philistine. Goliath should have known then what he was up against, but he was foolish and blind. David then activated the supernatural power of God by telling Goliath, "This day will the Lord deliver thee into mine hand, and I will smite thee, and take thine head from thee; and I will give the carcasses of the host of the Philistine this day unto the fowls of the air, and to the wild beasts of the earth; that all the earth may know that there is a God in Israel" 1 Samuel 17:46 (KJV). David definitively said, "Today is your last day; no longer will you torment the armies of *my* God."

The words we speak, good—bad are activated into the atmosphere, hemisphere and stratosphere—celestial and terrestrial. We must be careful not to speak "capricious" words.

Capricious words are negative and self-defeating declarations. Superstitious, myths, and fables have no power and bear no truth if we trust and believe the Word of God. Listed below are self-defeating proclamations:

- When it rains, it pours
- How bad can it get
- I am broke
- Today is not my day

Superstitions

- Don't split the pole
- Don't put your purse on the floor, because you will not have any money
- If my hand itches, I am getting money
- If a spider hangs from his web before me, a stranger is coming to my home
- Bad luck if I break a mirror or cross before a black cat

Superstition began centuries ago. Some believe that it was birthed from our ancestors attempting to explain mysterious circumstances as best they could with the knowledge they had.

The dictionary defines superstition as an irrational and often quasi-religious belief in and reverence for the magical effects of some actions and rituals, or the magical powers of some objects. It is also defined as a deep-seated belief that good or bad luck will result from performing it.

On the contrary, our success and prosperity is not determined by luck, but by the favor and blessings of the Lord. Our thoughts as well as our speech should be of virtue and a good report. These are just a few examples; I could list several more. The author Paul writes in the book of Philippians 4:8 (KJV) "Finally, brethren, whatsoever things *are* true, whatsoever things *are* honest, whatsoever things are just, whatsoever things *are* pure, whatsoever things *are* lovely, whatsoever things *are* of a good report; if there be any virtue, and if there be any praise think on these things." The mind is powerful. Our character and conduct begin with the mind. Our actions are governed by our thoughts. Hence, our minds must be renewed daily. The book of Proverbs talks about pleasant words. "Pleasant words *are* as an honeycomb, sweet to the soul, and health to the bones." 16:24 (KJV)

James the brother of Jesus and author of the book of James talks about the tongue and says that life and death are in the power of the tongue. Let's examine this more extensively. David had a bag of five smooth stones; the number five represents grace. God's unmerited favor was upon David. When you have the favor of God, it really doesn't matter what you have or don't have. Grace supersedes the laws of science, policies, and contracts. I know this because; both, my husband and I have obtained jobs and positions before obtaining the degree. Though the policy manual and requirements for the job indicated a master's degree was needed, my husband was hired for the job. Though my salary and responsibilities required a master's degree, I was called and hired for the job. This is what we call efficacious grace—it goes beyond common grace. It is unmerited, undeserved, and unearned favor; being in the right place at the right time. Efficacious grace enables God to assert power over time and space. The Greek word *kairos* denotes a critical juncture—God's time, which is real time, interrupts, chronological time. The Greek word is *chromos*—

watch time—*a divine* appointment is setup. Time and place meet up together. Awesomely, everything works in your favor. Codes and regulations are in your favor; they change for you and me.

Romans chapter 4 tells us that David and Abraham were justified by faith. In verse 17 (KJV), Paul writes " … before him whom he believed, even God, who quickeneth the dead, and calleth those things, which be not as though they were." Paul also quotes Genesis 17:5, KJV as a reference. "Neither shall thy name any more be called Abram, but thy name shall be Abraham; for a father of many nations have I made thee."

God is speaking of what is yet to take place—yet has already happened. It is a promise of certainty-spoken 25-years before Abraham would witness the birth of Isaac. Paul wants to illustrate that the foundation of Abraham was already set.

God calls things that are not according to our perspective, into existence. This is not trickery of revelation. Christ himself already set the foundation. He quickens the dead things and brings life. At an old age, Abraham was still able to produce life.

The promise was already established that all things would work together for the good of them who love God and are called according to his design and purpose. God foreknew David—he predestinated him and called him. Because David responded in humbled obedience, he was justified and declared righteousness—whom God justifies he glorifies. God knows those who want to know him. He predestinates them to become believers and thereby they are called to serve, declared righteous and are glorified (Romans 8:28–30, KJV).

To prove this we can look at Ecclesiastes 3:14–15 (AMP).

> "I know that whatever God does, it endures forever; nothing can be added to it nor anything taken from it. And God does it so, that men will [reverently] fear Him [revere and worship Him, knowing that He is] That which is now already has been, and that which is to be, already has been: and God seeks that which has passed by [so that history repeats itself]."

David was already glorified. The promise of victory was already established. David's part was to appropriate the Word of God by operating in faith. He knew that faith was not trying but trusting—not behaving but believing. Therefore, he used what he had—five smooth stones and he only needed to release one through his slingshot. That one stone was the multiplication of power. With the first four, he took authority and released them into the atmosphere; he proclaimed the outcome before he put the fifth stone in the slingshot. His proclamation impelled the circumstance before him to change in his favor. Furthermore, he imposed the Word of God on Goliath, which set everything in motion. The one small stone slung by David settled in Goliath's head and forced him to the ground, facedown. Though he fell to the ground, he wasn't dead. David took Goliath's sword and severed his head. Goliath did not realize it, but he was subject to David's authority.

Two points should be emphasized here:

- David already won the battle before he spoke the words or used the slingshot. The favor of God was upon him. Therefore, everything was already in his favor

- David walked in his kingly anointing. Goliath was delivered into his hands *before* the stone was slung. He declared these things:

  - This day, will the Lord deliver thee into mine hand (today is your last day to torment)

  - I will smite thee (I will slice and cut off your head)

  - I will give the carcasses of the host of the Philistine this day unto the fowls of the air; and the wild beasts of the earth (there will be nothing left of you)

  - that all the earth may know that there is a God in Israel (the testimony of God will be known today)

    (1 Samuel 17:46 KJV)

If I had to argue whether the other four stones were used, my summation would be that David canceled Goliath's ill spoken words, threats, and coercions by pronouncing the Word of God. Therefore, he did use the other four stones by diatribe activation. Like David, every battle is training ground for future battles. Though you may have been in a few battles and you may have suffered a few bruises, you are still here. Hallelujah!

Nevertheless, God can heal and erase all scars. You are reading this book today because you have withstood the past, and now it is time to move forward. There is some executing to be performed and we will need to be audacious just like David. We will execute the giants who come to torment and delay the process of God in our lives. Our weapons are the Word of God and the prayer of legislation, which delivers the devil into our hand, enabling us the power to sever his head. What does this mean? *His lifeline is cut off.*

SPIRITUALLY strong

AN OPEN DOOR

Many have asked, "Why do bad things happen to good people? If God is who he says he is, then why was I exposed to such pain and grief?" We have to look at Genesis to answer these questions.

> "The Lord God planted a garden eastward in Eden: and there he put the man whom he had formed. And out of the ground made the Lord God to grow every tree that is pleasant to the sight, and good for food; the tree of life also in the midst of the garden, and the tree of knowledge of good and evil."
>
> (Genesis 2:8–9, KJV)

Adam and Eve were in heaven's prefecture—a sequestered garden. They dwelled in the presence of God in a delightful garden east of Eden. They were placed in his presence, where there was fullness of joy and pleasures forevermore extended from his right hand to them. Adam was to cultivate and preserve the garden from all intruders. The Hebrew word for keep is *shamar,* meaning to hedge about the ground, or protect. Adam was allowed to eat of every tree, even the tree of life. However, God gave specific instructions not to eat of the tree of knowledge of good and evil.

The serpent beguiled Eve, and she became the first to violate the divine regulations governing their lives. However, because Adam was given direct instructions, the Word of God holds Adam as the disobedient one. Knowing what the instructions were, he broke trust with God.

Nevertheless, the violation does not imply that she was less intelligent or more vulnerable to deception than Adam was, but by Satan's insidious plan, man fell, and deception of the woman preceded active disobedience of the man. When Adam disobeyed God, Satan became the pseudo-ruler of the earth. Adam's body took on corruption, leading to death and the grave. Sickness, evil, and devastation were all wrapped up in the tree of knowledge. Man learned that he was naked, but his payoff was separation from God.

The following led and contributed to the fall of man:

- Adam and Eve doubted God's Word

- Satan embellished and misquoted God's Word

- God's Word was misinterpreted

God never intended for Adam, Eve, or man to experience pain, sickness, or corruption. The sin and disobedience of Adam and Eve proliferated sin and sickness in the human race and thereby Adam and Eve suffered loss. The Bible tells us that after the fall of man, man slowly deteriorated in time. Before the flood, man's average life span was 900 years.

- Adam lived for 930 years (Genesis 5:5)
- Enosh lived 905 years (Genesis 5:11)
- Methuselah lived 969 years (Genesis 5:27)
- Noah lived 950 years (Genesis 9:29)

After the flood, the average life span dropped rapidly, then gradually leveled off. The following covers a time span of twenty-three generations.

- Shem lived 960 years (Genesis 11:11)
- Eber lived 464 years (Genesis 11:16)
- Abraham lived 175 years (Genesis 25:7)
- Jacob lived 147 years (Genesis 47:28)
- Joseph lived 110 years (Genesis 50:22)

Before the redemption of Christ, man lost much in the fall.

- Spiritual, physical and eternal life (Isaiah 59:2; Romans 5:12–21; Ephesians 2)
- Communion with God (Isaiah 59:2)
- Fellowship with animals (Genesis 9:2)

- His full dominion over all things (Psalms 8)
- Liberty from Satan (John 12:40; 2 Corinthians 4:4; Ephesians 6:10–18; Revelations12:9)
- Perfect God-consciousness (Genesis 2:25; 3:7)
- Complete power to do good (Genesis 6: 5–7; Romans 7)
- Seamless self-control (Ephesians 2; Galatians 5)
- Right to the tree of life (Genesis 3:22–24)
- Garden home (Genesis 2:15; 3:22–24)
- God's glory (Romans 3:23)
- Righteousness and true Holiness (Ephesians 4:22–24)
- All benefits of perfect union with God (Revelations 21: 1–7; 22:1–3)
- Perfect health (Genesis 3:16–19; Matthew 8:17; 1 Peter 2:24)

Adam and Eve opened a door that could not be closed until Jesus took our sins by taking up the cross. He took our sins, and we gained eternal life, perfect healing, and wholeness. What an incredible symbol of divine grace that God—in his mercy and in his giving of the first promise of a Messiah—the Lord chose to bring about this seed through the woman.

Concisely, the one first blemished by sin is selected to be the one first promised to become an instrument of God's redemptive work. This gives us a glimpse of perfect healing and the power of deliverance.

The enemy seeks whom he may devour, to sift as wheat, waiting to thrash and winnow his prey into desert places. He desires to cause separation from God—that you find yourself on unfamiliar soil. The unfamiliar soil is the wilderness, wasteland, and a harsh environment. We can look at the scripture below; that clearly tells us we were sought out. The book of Job tells us,

> "And the Lord said unto Satan, Whence comest thou? Then Satan answered the Lord, and said From going to and fro in the earth, and from walking up and down in it."
>
> (Job 1:7, KJV)

Satan conspires to devour whom he can. This is what he does every day, every minute. Satan and his evil forces are the agents of destruction, not God. The only sense in which God destroys is to withhold his protection and thereby turn an individual over to the devil to carry out his work upon that person; this is generally because of disobedience. Many times, because of sin and rebellion, God used the Israelites' enemies to bring them into captivity. When the Israelites repented, God delivered them. Isaiah chapters 42–45 demonstrate how after repentance God does deliver:

> "Thus said the Lord, thy redeemer, and he that formed thee from the womb, I *am* the Lord that maketh all *things;* that stretcheth forth the heavens alone, that spreadeth abroad the earth by myself; That frustrateth the tokens of the liars,

and maketh diviners mad; that turneth wise *men* backward, and maketh their knowledge foolish, That confirmeth the word of his servant, and performeth the counsel of his messengers; that saith to Jerusalem, Thou shalt be inhabited; and to the cities of Judah, Ye shall be built, and I will raise up the decayed places thereof; That said to the deep, Be dry, and I will dry up thy rivers: That saith of Cyrus, *He* is my shepherd, and shall perform all my pleasure; even saying to Jerusalem, Thou shalt be built, and to the temple, Thy foundation shall be laid" (Isaiah 44:24–28, KJV).

"Thus Saith the Lord to his anointed, to Cyrus, whose right hand I have holden, to subdue nations before him; and I will loose the loins of the kings, to open before him the two leaved gates; and the gates shall not be shut: I will go before thee, and make the crooked places straight: I will break in peaces the gates of brass and cut in sunder the bars of iron: And I will give thee treasures of darkness, and hidden riches of secret places, that thou mayest know that I, the Lord, which call thee by thy name, *am* the God of Israel"
(Isaiah 45: 1–3, KJV).

Again, the Israelites were in captivity because of their obstinate disobedience. The prophet Isaiah tells them they are not forgotten and Judah will be restored. Over one hundred years later, God keeps his promise and uses Cyrus who Isaiah named as an instrument to subdue the nations before them and loose the armor of the king. Cyrus devised a diversion through the water channels. The gates of the inner walls of Babylon leading to the river were of brass. The outer walls were 100 feet high. These brass gates of Babylon were kept locked with bars of iron. Even great iron plates covered them in some places. However, on this night they carelessly left them open. Cyrus and his troops went under the high walls and walked through the two-leaved gates—they defeated the enemy. Pliny the Elder records that Cyrus took his conquest—hidden treasure as the Lord had promised, which amounted $353,427,200 (Chapter 45). What a triumph for the people of Israel.

The book of Job is an epic scriptural story demonstrating the case of Job—a rich man living in the land of Uz, located south of Edom and west of Arabia, extending to the borders of Chaldea. Job was afflicted in the body and his family and belongings were destroyed. He was the third son of Issachar, the son of Jacob.

According to the Nomadic people, it was customary to estimate wealth by the number of animals someone owned (Genesis 13:2, 5; 24:35). Job was blameless and upright, pious, and gracious to family and friends. He was a wealthy man in possession of 7,300 camels; 7,000 oxen; and 500 asses—a total estimated value of $790,000 (Job 1:3; 43:12, KJV).

Job, a Gentile, knew God by the name of *Shaddai*—"the Almighty" and the Lord called Job "His servant." The scripture attest that Job was a real person; it is a portrayal of his unfeigned faithfulness to God. God permitted the suffering, struggle, and sorrow of a real life to prove the integrity and triumphant victory of those who love and serve Him. The Bible records these happenings before the exodus from Egypt. Job's affliction lasted months. The details of his circumstances serve primarily to underscore the failed plot of Satan. What the devil meant for evil—God turned into good.

Satan, who is neither omnipresent nor omniscient, challenged the piety of Job. He could not truly determine the outcome of his egregious attack. If he only knew Job's relationship with God, he may have looked for another vessel. When Satan attacked Job, he had a plan. It is important to understand that Satan is responsible for bringing about the actual happenings of accidents, sickness, disease, and calamity—all specific spirits we will cover in chapter five.

Once Satan has brought about such mishaps and violent acts, he warps the thinking of man to believe that God is the one behind the scenes who has brought such things to pass. Generally, those who have suffered from the effects of the devil falsely blame these works on God. Don't think it strange, but even some Christians who are taught the Word of God blame God.

Satan's attack on Job was to prove his hypothesis—that no man will serve God without personal gain. Satan wanted to prove that if God will not bless man financially, physically, etc., then man would automatically curse and hate him. The Bible proves this untrue, for millions have loved and served God without such personal material gain.

When God authorizes the work of Satan, it is to

bring deliverance. It is never for the work of destruction. On the other hand, Satan's work is for destruction. As Job had, we have a hedge around us (Job 1:10). Whatever you are going through, you can trust that the Lord is allowing it to happen. However, if we chose to live life on our own, without a relationship with God, we are open prey to the enemy.

> "And the children of Israel did evil in the sight of the Lord: and the Lord delivered them into the hand of Midian seven years. And the hand of Midian prevailed against Israel: *and* because of the Midianites, the children of Israel made them the dens, which *are* the mountains, and caves, and strong holds. And *so* it was, when Israel had sown, that the Midianites came up against them; And the Amalekites, and the children of the east, even they encamped against them, and destroyed the increase of the earth, till thou come unto Gaza, and left no sustenance for Israel, neither sheep, or ox, nor ass. For they came up with their cattle and their tents, and they came as grasshopper for multitude; *for* both they and their camels were without number: and they entered into the land to destroy it. And Israel was greatly impoverished because of the Midianites; and the children of Israel cried unto the Lord. And it came to pass, when the children of Israel cried unto the Lord because of the Midianites, That the Lord sent a prophet unto the children of Israel, which said unto them, Thus saith the Lord God of Israel, I brought you up from Egypt, and brought you forth out of the house of bondage. And I deliv-

ered you out of the hand of the Egyptians, and out of hand of all that oppressed you and drave them out from you, and gave them their land. And I said unto you, I *am* the Lord your God; fear not the gods of the Amorites, in whose land ye dwell: but ye have not obeyed my voice. And there came an angel of the Lord, and sat under an oak which was in Ophrah, that *pertained* unto Joash the Abi-ezrite: and his son Gideon threshed wheat by the winepress, to hide it from the Midianites. And the angel of the Lord appeared unto him, and said unto him, The Lord *is* with thee, thou mighty man of valour. And Gideon said unto him, Oh my Lord, if the Lord be with us, why then is all this befallen us? And where be all his miracles, which our fathers told us of, saying. Did not the Lord bring us up from Egypt? But now the Lord hath forsaken us, and delivered us into the hands of the Midianites. And the Lord looked upon him, and said, Go in this thy might, and thou shalt save Israel from the hand of the Midanites: have not I sent thee? And he said unto him, Oh my Lord, wherewith shall I save Israel? Behold, my family is poor in Manasseh, and I am the least in my father's house. And the Lord said unto him, Surely I will be with thee, and thou shalt smite the Midianites as one man."

(Judges 6:1–17, KJV)

The book of Judges demonstrates how the Israelites turned away from God, but because of their repentance, God raised up Gideon to defeat the Midianites. Israel had a recurring pattern of apostasy in the sight of God. Many times, the Lord used the Babylonians—their enemy, a heathen nation that worshiped other gods—and others to attack Israel only to get their attention. Many times, they cried out in repentance to the Lord, and the Lord delivered them.

The Door Was Left Open

Satan comes to abort innocence—the mission is to cause death and shame. I was an innocent little girl, premeditated prey to the demonic forces of this world sought out by spiritual wickedness in high places. Though God, my maker, breathed the breath of life into me, the enemy's intent was to suffocate the will of God out of my life. From a baby in a playpen to a toddler trying to take my first step in this overwhelming and confusing world, I was already victimized—or so the devil thought. I was helpless and dependent on my parents to protect and nurture me. During my childhood development, I was under attack.

American Baby Magazine reports that babies do not have specific memories. A baby's long-term memory can extend back twenty-four hours at six weeks old and up to four times that at sixteen months old.

This explains why I am confident that my molestation began while I was still young enough to be in the playpen. However, I am not sure when it happened for the first time or how old I was. What is clear is that I was a cuddly baby, innocent, and precious before the Lord. God breathed the breath of life—or the Hebrew word *ruwach*—into me, and I was full of life and full of destiny. Though I came through my mother's loins, it was God who gave me life. I am reminded of Adam, formed from the dust of the earth to a lump of clay. When he received *neshamah,* or the breath of God, he became a living and breathing image of God. This is personal to me.

The door was left open, allowing spiritual wickedness access to my family and me. Spiritual wickedness in high places is mentioned in Ephesians 6:12. Also known by the Greek phrase "*pneumatikos poneria epouranios,*" these spirits are responsible for anything that is perverted, depraved, debased, warped, or corrupt. The door was left open, and the strong man entered.

In the New Testament, Luke writes, "When the strong man armed keepeth his palace, his goods are in peace: But when a stronger than he shall come upon him, and overcome him, he taketh from him all his armor wherein he trusted, and divideth his spoils" Luke 11:21–22 (KJV).

The AMP says it like this: "When the strong, fully armed, guards his own dwelling, his belongings are undisturbed. But when one stronger than he attacks him and conquers him, he robs him of his whole armor on which he relied and divides up *and* distributes all his goods as plunder."

My father was the strong man. He was not my biological father, but since I never knew the seed bearer, this man was the only father I knew. He was obviously a sick man who had succumbed to the demonic forces of unclean spirits. There was no peace in my house. The man had entered and plundered the goods of my house. The enemy was living in the camp, and for many years, he was never detected. His camouflage was image and perception—a delusion. He portrayed to be something that he wasn't. The incomprehensible truth of this man was concealed for years. As the devil does, he imitated a life of prosperity and normalcy.

This masquerade gave the illusion of a prestigious businessman who worked his way up from custodian to company representative, who in the seventies drove a brand new company car each year. Yearly, he took his family—seven girls and wife—on vacations that were rare for a middle-class family.

Many accepted the mask. They only viewed a homeowner with a rock garden in the front yard, a manicured lawn, a pool with a slide, and monkey bars in the backyard. The charade was sealed by the image of the American dream—a white, picket fence and Ginger the toy poodle running around in the yard. My mom, neighbors, family, friends and co-workers were all beguiled.

Unfamiliar Territory

My family suffered much, because an intruder came to interrupt the innocence of seven girls. This predator came to violate the people closest to him. Years later, I learned that all of my sisters were victims of molestation, incest, and physical and verbal abuse. The predator was cunning; he individually attacked them in order to keep them in seclusion, captive to him and powerless to each other. Consequently, no one ever talked about the abuse. We were in pain, but we didn't talk about it. We were emotionally and psychologically unstable, but we did not talk about it.

Driven away from each other, we moved to other states, and still, we did not talk about it.

Though my sisters and I physically moved out of the house; subconsciously, we never left the house. The craftiness and ultimate plan of Satan was to separate us from God and move each one of us into unfamiliar territory. We were spiraling down into a bottomless pit—a pit of desperation, depression, instability, and sickness.

Not only did my sisters and I suffer great loss, but my mother—a woman who wanted nothing more than to give her girls the best. This predator physically and mentally abused her. The violent abuse began before some of my sisters were even born. The enemy's scheme was two-fold, giving a false sense of stability, sufficiency, and then dependency; she came to totally fear and depend on him.

First, he became her source of income; he paid all of her bills, gave her money for household needs, and allowed her authorization for credit cards. She didn't have a driver's license so he was in total control—driving her to each store. Subsequently, he physically and mentally abused her, which caused her to fear him. For years, she was powerless to him. He wanted to ensure she was emotionally and physiologically captive, and so throttled by her own pain that she could not be the refuge for the girls she birthed and nurtured. She was looking for her own refuge and a way out.

Genesis 3:1 says, "Now the serpent was more subtle *and* crafty than any living creature of the field which the Lord God had made" (AMP).

Let's examine this. Moses, the writer, intends for us to notice that the serpent is more cunning than any other beast of the field—the head of the animals. Here are some facts we should know about the serpent.

The beast of the field	Had reasoning power
More cunning than all other	Had knowledge of God's plan
Created by God	Head of the animals
A serpent, which is the devil	Capable of hostility and enmity
Had power of speech	Close to man in Eden
Had illusory powers	Cursed above all animals

The Hebrew word for serpent *nahash* in Genesis 3:1 occurs 31 times in 28 verses in the Hebrew concordance KJV; however, it remains under debate whether it means a literal serpent or warrior-like-abilities. Conversely, a reference scripture, Revelation 12:9 (KJV) also records the word serpent *ophis*, which regarded by the latter Jews as the devil (Strong's G-3789).

Satan is a fallen angel who narrated to Eve a sly interpretation of God's Word. His calculated plan was to speak enough to seduce Eve's natural curiosity. Because of sin, and their conscious decision to disobey God, Adam and Eve were sent away—cast out of the garden into unfamiliar territory. The garden was the place of their unique communion with God. Now, cherubim were wielding swords, assuring that they would bring death if Adam and Eve tried to return.

> "And the Lord God said, Behold the man is become as one of us, to know good and evil: and now, lest he puts forth his hand, and take also of the tree of life, and eat, and live forever; Therefore, the Lord God sent him forth from the Garden of Eden, to till the ground from whence he was taken. So he drove out the man; and he placed at the east of the Garden of Eden Cherubim, and a flaming sword, which turned every way to keep the way of the tree of life."
>
> (Genesis 3:22–24, KJV)

Again, this explains why it was *you*, why it was my sisters and family, why it was me, and why many children are victims. As we see, this was the plot since the beginning of time. Nevertheless, we are heirs to God and joint heirs to Jesus. The promise of God is alive in our lives. No matter the plot, we are spiritually strong. We are victorious.

THE MATURATION PROCESS

As you read in the previous chapter, Satan's purpose is to leave you homeless and Fatherless. Here, I want to focus on the victims' early stages of childhood, since this is generally when a predator attacks. The maturation is the processes of becoming mature—the attainment of emotional and intellectual maturity. During these precious stages of development, when our trust, autonomy, industry, identity, and coordination are advancing, the enemy's organized plan is to dominate and restrict our every movement. His desire is to be the puppeteer of our lives, with strings extended to our heads, limbs, and feet and to other areas—self-esteem, family, and spirit. Psychologically, he can then control our every movement.

The horrific violation of sexual abuse is on the rise. This crime has infected cyberspace, which is the portal to our homes, children and love ones. The cases are insurmountable. There are statistics to prove my claim. The number of childhood abuse and molestation cases increases every year. According to the Charles Keating of Citizens for Decency through law, research reveals that roughly thirty-three percent of girls and fourteen percent of boys are molested before the age of eighteen, according to the United States Department of Justice. Nearly two-thirds of all sexual assaults reported involved minors, and roughly, one-third involved children under the age of twelve. In most cases, however, child molestation goes unreported. The FBI estimates that only thirty-seven percent of all rapes are reported to the police. The Bureau of Justice, National Criminal victimization survey 1996 statistics are lower, thirty percent reported the crime. Kids are often frightened or embarrassed, and many times, they do not say anything. The predator's objective is to attack during the dependency and development stages—the maturation process.

Child development refers to biological and psychological changes that occur in human beings and the end of adolescent. Developmental change may occur as a result of genetically controlled processes known as maturation, or because of environmental factors and learning, most commonly involved in interaction. When a baby is born, he has experienced the first stage of development. During the first five years of life, a child will gain independence, mobility, speech and language, and he or she will develop a unique personality. The developmental stage is the most crucial time for a baby's development. If any of these skills and senses are not properly developed, the child will suffer certain insufficiencies, and normal growth is not possible. Let's take a closer look at the developmental stages.

Infant Stage

Trust and or mistrust are developed at this stage. Also at this state, the infant requires maximum comfort, protection, and tender love and care. These things or the lack thereof, can determine whether the child will grow to trust or mistrust others. Motor skills are also developed—body, posture, and large movements of the limbs pave the road to walking and the ability to perform other complex movements.

Toddler Stage

This is the stage where manipulative skills, which include complicated manual tasks, fine motor skills, and small movements are developed—crawling, walking, kicking, and grabbing. In this stage, either autonomy—shame, and or doubt are formed. It is the development to physically function and master in the environment while maintaining self-esteem.

Preschooler Stage

During this stage conscience and sexual identity are developed. Children develop initiative and begin to initiate activities. Pre-kindergartners benefit from experiences that support the development of fine motor skills in the hands and fingers, and where movements like writing and tying shoes are developed at this stage. Speech, language, and hearing are developed. If not nurtured in a healthy and supporting environment, low self-esteem could develop.

School—age Stage

This stage entails the development of the personal and social self and interactions with others. It is also, where skills for a healthy sense of self-worth are refined.

Adolescent Stage

Our identity is established, but there is often identity or role confusion. In this stage, we learn to integrate many roles—child, sibling, student, athlete, and worker—into a complete self-image by observing role models and handling peer pressure.

Young Adult Stage

We learn personal commitments at this stage. It is in this stage either intimacy or isolation develops within the personality.

Middle-aged Adult

This is the stage wherein we seek satisfaction through productivity in career, family, and civic interests. At this state, generally, stagnation could develop.

Older Adult

At this stage, we will review our life accomplishments and deal with loss.

Based on our review, we could either live in despair or we can live with great integrity.

Pedophiles and Molesters

Now that we understand the maturation process, let's examine the important difference between pedophiles and molesters. It is important to understand that public presentation tells us nothing about pedophiles or molesters. Their private lives are hidden. They are careful to look into your eyes just long enough to make you comfortable—shake your hand with just enough strength so that you are comfortable.

The term "pedophilia" refers to a persistent attraction or feeling in an adult or older adolescent to prepubescent children. A person with these tendencies is a pedophile. Pedophilia is a psychological disorder that does not necessarily require or involve a criminal act. The pedophile may never go public or share his fantasies; he might keep his desires a secret. Pedophiles have been known to marry single mothers to gain access to their children. Pedophiles can be very determined and single-minded in their efforts to stay close to children. Maintaining access, to children at all costs is one of the defining trademarks of pedophilia.

There are two types of molesters often discussed: the *situational* child molester and the *preferential* child molester. The situational child molester engages in sex for a variety of reasons and it has nothing to do with a sexual origin or desire. They do not possess a genuine sexual preference for children. Rather, the motivational factors are criminal in nature. The child molester has often suffered some type of abuse—generally, mistreated by friends, colleagues, and family. They are of low self-esteem and maintain poor moral standards.

Preferential child molesters have a sexual preference for children and usually maintain these desires throughout their lives. Though they can have an astounding number of victims, their crimes can remain undiscovered for many years. Preferential child molesters are strategic. Their behavior is predictable; they will befriend children and seduce them with gifts appealing to their emotional weaknesses.

Child molestation happens in every part of society and often happens in the early developmental ages. Children are most at risk from the adults in their own family and from the adults who are in their parents' social circles. In fact, ninety percent of abusers target children in their own families and children who they know well.

The National Alert Registry reports that one out of every three to four girls has been sexually assaulted by the age of eighteen. One boy out of every six will be abused by the age of eighteen. Though they have some reports on which to base these statistics, they are actually not accurate. So many cases of child molestation go unreported each year, so we really cannot estimate the real numbers. The FBI reports that The National Alert Registry of National Institute of Mental Health found only one percent to ten percent of victims ever tell that they were abused. Boys report far less than girls.

- The average child molester will molest 50 girls before being caught and convicted

- A child molester who seeks out boys will molest 150 boys before being caught and convicted, and he will commit at least 280 sexual crimes in his lifetime

- The average pedophile will commit 117 sexual crimes in his lifetime

- Most sexual abuse happens between the ages of seven and thirteen

- There are over 4,000 registered sex offenders in the United States

- People known by the family or victim are the most common abusers. The acquaintance molester accounts for 70–90% of reported cases

The social reaction to the problem of sexual offending has heightened. It is also important to mention that pedophiles and child molesters serve the least amount of time compared to murderers. According to the 1991 Bureau Justice Statistics survey of inmates, murderers serve an average sentence of 381 months, robbery is 200 months, and sexual assault is 211 months. Most prisoners, in general, are expected to serve about half of the time. Prison has a revolving door, and pedophiles and child molesters are among the first to be released. Often they come out and commit the same crimes again. According to the United States Department of Justice, on any given day, there are approximately 234,000 sex offenders who were convicted of rape or sexual assaults and in the custody or control of correction agencies.

This explains the high rate of repeated child abuse in our society. Children could be at risk of child abuse in the early, crucial stages of development. Society tends to put more emphasis on little girls, but we must understand that boys are also at risk, and more of their cases go unreported.

The Protector

Parents must be cognizant of the signs of possible abuse. These signs could include depression, which leads to seclusion, instability, fear, nightmares, identity crises, and personality conflicts. Child molesters and predators are generally those who are close to their victims or to their victims' family and this makes it hard for children to come forward. For years, I was afraid to tell my mother about the abuse. I was told that she would not believe me and would hate me. I was helpless and in fear.

I fostered an open relationship in raising my children, so they would feel comfortable sharing their concerns and problems with me. My husband and I taught them the Word of God and to always speak the truth, because the truth holds to the end. As Martin Luther King once said, "Truth crushed to the ground will rise again."

Though we attended church and were committed to God and the ministry, we had our own Bible study on Thursday evenings as well. We fasted as a family—even our pets. We ate dinner together without the interruption of the telephone or TV. Every morning, I anointed my children's head with the anointed oil, and we joined hands to pray before anyone left to go to school or work. When one of us was sick, we proclaimed healing.

The blood of Jesus hovered over our home; the anointing destroyed every yoke and kept my children safe and out of harm's way. This does not mean that my family did not experience any trials, tribulation, or afflictions. There were many along the way, but God kept us as a family—we were always safe in his hands. He always delivered and healed. We experienced his miracles, and—so you know that I have not gone off on a tangent—he broke the curse from which I suffered. My children, their children, and their children's children will never have to suffer from sexual abuse.

My husband was the alpha male, but I was also a protector—the beta. We have always been a team— we are one, or *echad.* There are certain things we did not allow. Our children were not allowed to sleep elsewhere, even with family. We never liked the idea of slumber parties until the children were older. I have had my own bad experiences, which are still fresh in my mind. I would not allow myself to be ignorant to the devil's devices.

When I was a teenager, my mom allowed her friend's daughter to sleep over, and she was assigned to sleep in my bed with me. It was late, and we had called it a night. I shared a bedroom with two of my sisters. We turned the lights off, and everyone was on their way to sleep. I am not sure what came over my friend, but she tried to get on top of me. With much force, I pushed her off of me and scurried to find the lamp switch on my night table. It was dark, and I hit the bottom of my chin and split it open on the corner of the table. I still have the scar today. Enough said about that episode. Just know that she never slept over again.

It is important that we are aware of the devil's devices. Parents must be the protectors. In some cases, a prepubescent child is curious and may fondle another child. It could be as innocent as playing doctor or acting like mommy and daddy. These acts should be handled with care and caution. Talk to your children with a calm voice. Communicate with them, and explain why they should not fondle each other.

Parents should be aware of a more serious epidemic. In the last ten years, sexual abuse among children is on the rise—child-on-child sex abuse. It refers to a form of child abuse in which a prepubescent child is sexually abused by one or more children or adolescent youths, and in which no adults is directly involved. This type of abuse occurs without consent, but by force, trickery, and or emotional manipulation. This is different from "playing doctor"—there is a deliberate action directed at sexual stimulation of orgasm.

Fifty percent of children who have been abused also become predators. Facilities for these offenders are full; most often, the beds are not empty. These are young boys and girls who are on the prowl for other children—family, friends, and even schoolmates. The parents of these afflicted children are often totally uninformed and distraught when it surfaces that their children are the victimizers.

Whether the child is the victim or the victimizer, prayer, counseling, and love are needed to bring about deliverance and healing. Trust has to be developed, and there has to be patience enough for the long haul. Healing can happen, but it doesn't happen overnight.

We must pray for change within the judicial system, starting with the lawmakers. If we believe in the need for a change, we can decree that the Lord will touch the hearts of the lawmakers in Congress to enact laws that will protect our children. This prayer speaks to the demonic forces of this world. We have power to ask that the Lord protect the children by covering them in the blood. Hallelujah!

CLOSE THE DOOR I

The door I am speaking of is a gateway—an entrance that the enemy uses to afflict families with poverty—abuse, and all manner of sickness. These are generational curses that must be identified in order for the door to be closed. Often times, generational curses go undetected and are never addressed; therefore, the door remains open. If we do not close the door by breaking the curses, as we will read further in the chapter, the enemy can still invade your territory and bring forth destruction; that moves from one generation to the next.

The Bible illustrates David as a man after God's own heart. He sinned, yet with a penitent heart, he went before the Lord to ask for forgiveness. His first recorded sins—indiscretions and toxic behavior—opened the door to the curses of incest, rape, and murder in 2 Samuel 11:2–25. While in the presence of the prophet Nathan, David repented to God of his sins; however, it did not exempt him from the penalties. The just and merciful God put away David's sin and did not allow death to be his punishment. Nevertheless, these were the penalties that came upon David and his house:

- A sword would never depart from his house
- His wives would be taken and given to his neighbors
- His child would die
- Evil would rise in his house
- His sins would be before man, and disgrace would come to his house

The Bible delineates the sin of rape and disgrace in the following verses.

"Absalom, the son of David, had a fair sister, whose name was Tamar; and Amnon [her half brother] son of David loved her. And Amnon was so troubled that he fell sick for his [half] sister Tamar, for she was a virgin, and Amnon thought it impossible for him to do anything to her. But Amnon had a friend, whose name was Jonadab, the son of Shimeah, David's brother, and Jonadab was a very crafty man. He said to Amnon, Why are you, the king's son, so lean and weak-looking from day to day? Will you not tell me? And Amnon said to him, I love Tamar, my [half] brother Absalom's sister. Jonadab said to him, Go to bed and pretend you are sick; and when your father David comes to see you, say to him, Let my sister Tamar come and give me food and prepare it in my sight, that I may see it and eat it from her hand. So Amnon lay down, and pretended to be sick; and when the king came to see him, Amnon said to the king, I pray you, let my sister Tamar come and make me a couple of cakes in my sight, that I may eat at her hand. Then David sent home and told Tamar, Go now to your brother Amnon's house, and prepare food for him. So Tamar went to her brother Amnon's house, and he was in bed. And she took dough and kneaded it and made cakes in his sight and did bake them. She took the pan and emptied it out before him, but he refused to eat. And Amnon said, Send everyone out from me. So everyone went out from him. Then Amnon said to Tamar, Bring the food here into the bedroom, so I may eat of your hand. So Tamar took the cakes she had made, and brought them into the room to Amnon her brother. And when she brought them to him, he took hold of her and said unto her, Come lie with me, my sister. She replied, No, my brother! Do not force *and* humble me, for no such thing should be done in Israel! Do not do this foolhardy, scandalous thing! And I, how could I rid myself of my shame? And you, you will be [considered] one of the stupid fools in Israel. Now therefore, I pray you, speak unto the king; for he will not withhold me from you. But he would not listen to her, and being stronger than she, he forced her and lay with her."

(2 Samuel 13:1–14, AMP)

The spirit of lust that was on David was now on his son Amnon. The unclean spirit entered his heart, enabling him to commit a vile act—an abomination before God. Lust was conceived, and Amnon fell sick; the devil took control of his mind, and over a short period, he ravished his half sister. Amnon plotted with his crafty and subtle cousin Jonadab a plan to have Tamar. Of whom does this remind us? Satan, the serpent who was crafty had the gumption to devise a plan to beguile the senses of a woman. Amnon, at twenty-two years old, was under the influence of the enemy (2 Samuel 11).

Tamar, whose name means palm tree, was fifteen years old—a beautiful, innocent creature. She was graceful, full of life, and lithesome like a palm tree—a virgin innocent who was kept in seclusion and away from men. She wore the colors of a virgin, which illustrated that she was being groomed to be a wife at the appointed time.

The story lets us know that Amnon deceived his father, which allowed Tamar entrance to his chambers to serve him. He had obviously appeared sick and had lost weight from not eating. Wickedness was upon him. Tamar was beguiled; without a doubt, she believed Amnon was sick. She entered his courts and innocently baked cakes and served him. While she was serving him, he asked everyone to leave and forced himself on her. This was a vile act; Tamar pleaded with Amnon and attempted to bring him to his senses. She reminded him of the shame that would be upon both of them if he committed such an act in Israel.

Tamar, who had no desire to marry her half brother, would have married him to prevent such a revolting act. She begged Amnon to speak to the king and ask to take her hand in marriage and save both of them from what was to come. Amnon was too cruel and beastly to listen. He violated her by forcing himself on her. The brutality of his act, along with his shame, remorse, and dread of punishment made him despise Tamar, and he ordered her out of his chambers. The righteousness in her was revolting to him. After the act of sin, he put her out and commanded his servant to bolt the door. The spirit of unnatural affection prevented Amnon from being the brother of protection but empowered him to be the predator.

Tamar was sent away in disgrace, perhaps a worse fate than rape. First, she suffered deception, then rape. Her innocence was robbed of her. To top it off, she was then rejected. What she once expected—to be known only by her husband—could no longer be a reality. Her beauty was turned to ashes. She could no longer wear the garment of many colors, which illustrated that a man had never touched her. Lust was conceived, and it did not stop until it brought forth the sins of rape and incest, which led to treason and death.

If you read further, you will see that David did not carry out the command of the law against Amnon, which was death. Consequently, rebellion came against him in his own house. Absalom hated his brother Amnon and waited two full years to kill him. Absalom went on to commit treason; he gave his allegiance to another king. Later, death came to him. Tamar was a desolate woman. David went before the Lord to petition that the curse be lifted that grace would abound.

Generational Curse

Generational curses are to be reckoned with. They do exist and operate in many families. Some of the curses extend from generation to generation. In my recent studies and teachings about generational curses, it is clear to me that many people, including Christians, do not have a comprehensive understanding of what generational curses are or how they operate. The Bible tells us in Matthew 11:12 that "the kingdom of heaven suffereth violence, and the violent take it by force" (KJV).

Clearly, many families have suffered violence due to generational curses, and these curses will continue to overtake the fabric of the family if nothing is done about them. The Bible tells us to stand in the power of God, who equips us with power and strength. The Amplified Bible says in the same verse as above that "the kingdom of heaven has endured violent assaults, and violent men seize it by force."

Since we have examined the curse upon David's family, let us deliberate the different kinds of curses. Satan desires to curse families with various forms

EMOTIONALLY WOUNDED SPIRITUALLY STRONG

of mental illness, or special physical illness, and he passes these down through the generations. The anatomies of a curse from Satan or his servants always involve demonic spirits. Satan is not only going after you; his object is not to afflict an individual, but the whole family line. The curse that is placed on a family is custom-made for that family. When a curse is placed, demonic spirits are sent to a person or family for a specific purpose. The sin of our forefathers can have a devastating effect on our own lives. I want to speak in real terms. Families and people fight; they battle, which can lead to hate. These behaviors often result in a curse being placed on the family unit or the whole family line.

There are three kinds of curses:

1. Curses from God
2. Curses from Satan and/or his servants with the legal right to curse
3. Curse from Satan and/or his servants without the legal right to curse

The first two types of curses can be broken only after repentance has occurred by those who were responsible for bringing them about.

Though David was a man after God's own heart, his plight was generational. He lusted after a married woman, Bathsheba, who conceived his child. To cover the sin, David had her husband killed. Think about it. What would Uriah have done if he found out? David felt he must cover up the sin. He was told before she was brought to him that she was married, but because of the lust of the eyes, lust of the flesh, and pride of life, he had to have her. After Bathsheba told David she was with child, he sent for her husband Uriah and insisted he come home from war and rest. David even sent a gift of food to his house, setting the scene. His intention was that Uriah, after seeing his wife, would desire to be with her for the evening, but that didn't happen. Uriah was so faithful to David and God that he refused to have one evening of comfort in his own bed or with his wife. David felt he had no other choice but to murder Uriah.

Sin caused the curse and the same spirits—lust, deception, and murder—to fall on the family. The curse was inflicted upon David's family because of disobedience, and it would have extended further if grace did not abound. Sin gives Satan authorization to release a curse. The Word of God lets us know that curses can extend for four generations if they are not broken.

> "For I the Lord thy God am a jealous God, visiting the iniquity of the fathers upon the children, unto the third and fourth *generation* of them that hate me;"
>
> (Exodus 20:5, KJV)

The repenting of a forefather's sin can break the second type of curse. Our ancestors may have been involved in things that they were not aware would release curses upon their families. My mom was in a clandestine organization for a few months. She had no idea that this was unacceptable to God and could open demonic doors on her family. I had another family member who was a bootlegger, and all of his sons dealt with drugs of some type. In order to close doors and break the curses, I went before the Lord to ask him to forgive them for their sins so that the generational curses on our family would be removed. Through prayer, fasting, touching, and agreeing with other family members, the curse was broken. Drugs, criminal activity, and mental illness began to cease, and my family members began to give their lives to the Lord.

The third type of curse is unauthorized by Satan; these are words spoken against a person—hexes, spells, and witchcraft. People can curse you by speaking ill things about you. If they don't like you, they can declare sickness on you by releasing words of destruction into the atmosphere. They can even release spells on objects and give them to you as gifts, with intent to harm you. I must tell you, have no fear. Ill-spoken words released into the atmosphere can be broken by the name of Jesus. We have the power to denounce what is in the atmosphere and replace these ill-spoken words with the Word of God.

The purpose of curses sent by Satan and his servants are always injury, loss, destruction, and often death. Curses sent by God are due to evil ways and rebellion. These curses are meant to get the recipient's attention and cause him to turn toward God so that his life is purified.

If you are experiencing the following, it could be possible that it is a curse.

- Everyone in the family dying of cancer
- Everyone dying at a certain age
- No one in the family coming to Christ
- Everyone in the family on drugs
- Everyone in the family in jail
- Everyone in the family is not in their right mind

The family line could also be characterized by particular problems.

- Divorce
- Poverty
- Uncontrolled anger/abuse
- Unbelief
- Crime

If you have prayed to break a curse and you or your family are still experiencing unsolved problems, you may be praying amiss, or perhaps you need another believer to touch and agree with you. Pray and ask the Holy Spirit to give you intervention. Let the Holy Spirit direct your prayer. Allow the Holy Spirit to reveal the source of the hindrance.

We can learn about family curses, blessings, and accomplishments if we talk with our family members. How many single-parent homes are you aware of today? Several, I am sure. Divorce is on the rise, even more frequently among Christians. Not only are mothers and fathers raising their children alone, but also grandparents are raising their grandchildren. Broken marriages are destroying any sense of heritage and continuity of family lines. Some of us know things about our grandparents, but very few of us have any knowledge beyond that. We know almost nothing about our family histories.

If people followed God's Word, they would be diligent about teaching their children the histories of their ancestors—both blessings and curses. This loss of knowledge seriously affects our lives, because we could learn from these experiences. In Leviticus 26:38–39, God tells the children all the terrible things that will happen to them when they turn away from serving him—famine, drought, and slaughter from invading armies.

Learning family history empowers and strengthens us. This is why it is important to understand our histories. Everything that is good and leaves a rich legacy should be shared to encourage the family. Everything associated with a curse should also be shared and dispelled. The curse must be replaced with declarations of education, wealth, prosperity, healing, wholeness, and salvation.

Sweeping the House

If my family history were shared with me, I probably would have had a clearer understanding of why my father abused his wife and daughters. This curse was passed down from generation to generation. Knowledge of my family's past would have enabled me to avoid many cultural and spiritual downturns in my life and family. It may have caused me to seek Jesus sooner. Nonetheless, I am now saved, and it is my responsibility in prayer and fasting to break the curses over my family. Creation was waiting for me to take my place.

In prayer, we are to build a formation that hedges our loved ones from the forces and snares of the enemy.

The gap, or *perets*, is the breaking place where we must stand in for those who are oppressed. Ezekiel 22:30 (KJV) says, "And I sought a man among them that should make up the hedge, and stand in the gap before me for the land, that I should not destroy it; but I found none." It is our responsibility to be strengthened and empowered by the Word of God, so we may stand in the gap for our families. If we don't, someone will not make it; they will decide to give up. Jesus came to do the will of the Father, and like Jesus, we were called to do the will of the Father.

Acts 10:38 says, "How God anointed Jesus of Nazareth with the Holy Ghost and with power: who went about doing good, and healing all that were oppressed of the devil; for God was with him" (KJV). Jesus Christ gave us the power to do so, and he expects us to use the authority given to us in his name.

Ask God to reveal what has cursed your family. Also ask God to forgive your forefathers of their sins. Ask the Lord to separate you from all the sins of your forefathers by the precious blood of Jesus. Ask the Lord to remove the curse. Satan then no longer has a legal right to curse you or your family. The Scripture tells us that if we confess the sins of our forefathers and do not walk contrarily to the Word of God, we will again be in covenant with God.

> "But if they confess their own and their fathers' iniquity in their treachery which they committed against Me—and also that because they walked contrary to Me. I also walked contrary to them and brought them into the land of their enemies—if then their uncircumcised hearts are humbled and they then accept the punishment for their iniquity. Then will I remember My covenant with Jacob, My covenant with Isaac, and My covenant with Abraham, and [earnestly] remember the land."
>
> (Leviticus 26:40–42, AMP)

Let's pray the curse is broken off of our families.

Lord, I thank you for Jesus. I thank you for allowing me to come into the understanding of curses and destiny power. For by you, I can run through troops, and by you, God, I can leap over walls. Your way is perfect! The Word of the Lord is tested and tried. God, you are a shield to all those who take refuge and put their trust in you. God, I stand in the gap today. You are the God who girds me

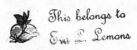

This belongs to
Eva L. Lemons

with strength and makes my way perfect. You make my feet like hinds feet, so that I am able to move swiftly as a deer above danger-ous height and trouble. Habakkuk 3:19. You secure my high places. You teach my hands to war, so that my arms can bend a bow of bronze. You have also given me the shield of your salvation, and your right hand has held me up. Your gentleness and kindness have made me great.

In the name of Jesus, Lord, I give you praise for revealing the curse of my family. I praise you for unveiling my eyes so that I may see into the spirit realm. Today, I pray for forgiveness for my forefathers. Lord, forgive them for all of their sins. Put their sins into a sea of forgetfulness, and remember them no more. Lord, forgive me for all of my sins, if I have opened any doors giving Satan authority to inflict my family and myself, thereby caus-ing generational curses. Forgive me. Close all doors my ancestors opened because of disobe-dience and rebellion. Father, forgive them.

Shake evil out of its place Lord. What the enemy meant for evil, turn into good. For your Word said you would make the crooked places straight. I bind the works of the enemy over my life. The *illusion* of wealth and prosperity is destroyed today. But every blessing with my name on it comes to me in the appointed time and season. There shall be no delays, substitutes or demonic encroachment. I decree that every yoke is destroyed. I am free, and my family is free from every curse. I proclaim that every chain is broken off of my life.

I command every euroclydon and blustering wind to cease. The spirit of incest, rape, and molestation is loosed off my family and destroyed today. I am smeared in the blood of the lamb; it covers every area of my life. Old things have passed away, and all things become new today. Not only am I healed, but also my family is healed from the stench of physical, physiological, and spiritual sickness. Every plot of the enemy has been canceled and I bind every clandestine spirit. The anointing that is upon me repels the enemy. The strong man cannot enter; there is a hedge and a firewall around me that cannot be penetrated. I walk in the blessing of my Lord, who is magnified in the prosperity of his saints. I seal this prayer in Jesus' name. Hallelujah!

Now that we have swept the house clean and asked for God's forgiveness for our sins and for our ancestors' sins, the door that was a gateway to these sins has been closed. The associated spirits have been bound, and the effects have been loosed off the family. Regardless of how it looks, continue to trust God, and plead the blood over your family. Continually praise God for the manifestation.

We will study this more in chapter five. Our families will not suffer the pain we had to endure. We can release this prayer into the atmosphere as we seal it with the blood of Jesus. Let's praise God for the miracle.

Prescription One

Because God has forgiven my sins and the sins of my forefathers, the curse over my family is broken.

CLOSE THE DOOR, PART II—THE FALLOW GROUND

We have shut some doors, and the healing process has begun, but in order for the injured and wounded to heal properly, the fallow ground must be broken up. Fallow ground is uncircumcised flesh and uncultivated soil—unfamiliar territory into which we were thrust. The ground is the surface dirt. Only weeds—undesirable and troublesome plants—grow profusely on this soil. As we've read, if the door is left open, the enemy can enter. He then has access to contaminate the once-rich soil and plant contaminated seeds. His sadistic acts take root and grow over the years.

Think of a tree that is rooted. It grew from a small bush into a large trunk that now reaches far past the rooftop of your home. The trunk is so wide that you can barely wrap your arms around it. Imagine trying to pull up the tree with your hands—it is impossible. Even if you used an electric saw to cut it down, the stump would still be in place. Because the stump is in place, it is still connected to the root, and the enemy has the authority to revisit whenever he pleases.

This is why the fallow ground—the uncircumcised soil—must be broken up. Fallow ground is hard—yet breakable. Breaking it up gives us access to the root so that it may be pulled up and destroyed. Satan sows corruptible seeds of doubt—thorns in hopes that they will take root and choke or destroy the life of any tangible Word you have received from God. The parable in Matthew 3:17 tells us that if we do not hear and believe the Word of God it then falls by the wayside—stony places and among thorns. Think of a treasure box buried under a slate of cement. It would be impossible to break up the cement with your bare hands; the correct tools are needed. Likewise, if abuse has gone on for a period of time, it will take much longer for the healing process to be completed. Typically, healing happens in stages. Therefore, we must chisel away at every addiction and all pain to get to the root; we must pull it up and destroy it.

A victim of abuse not only suffers tangible physical damage, but also emotional damage. If it is kept secret, within the confines of two or three family members, it has the ability to tear the fibers of the family apart, generation after generation. My sisters, because of shame and pain, never talked about the abuse. The generational curse had a foothold on the family; its roots went from us to our children. The silence gave the devil the authority to manifest himself and bring discord between sisters who could not understand each other's pain.

The devil left us senseless and in bondage, believing that we were stained with shame and guilt. In a situation like this, the devil speaks to the victims' spirit and tells them that what happened to them is partly their fault. This often happens when the perpetrator monetizes the act with gifts. If the acts happen during puberty, there is a chance that the victim will have mixed emotions. The victim may have hated it, but the body may have sometimes desired it. If it takes place for a period of time, the consciousness and senses, which are often blank during the abuse, are put on mute, forcing the mind to deal with the abuse.

The demon that afflicted my family was cunning, strategic and out of control. We were on vacation, visiting family and having fun, as families do. He attacked one of my sisters. Of course, he threatened her and told her not to say anything. The abuse was not just in the home; he would take one to the movies or to his job and try to lure them into the act. Another, he would pick up from school and find a place far away from everything.

For me, this happened until I was in my teens, until I had enough courage to fight back. When I did fight back, I was physically abused. Because of the abuse, I plotted to run away, though I had nowhere to go. Thank God, I stood my ground to end the abuse.

When abuse happens, regardless of what age, you fight yourself into adulthood and fault yourself. You believe that you contributed to the act. This is a normal response. I want you to know that it is okay to confess how you actually felt; this is the first step to healing. Suppressing such feelings is denial and prevents the healing process from beginning. You first have to acknowledge that it did happen.

Prescription Two

Repeat this confession: *It happened to me, and I am not ashamed.*

Romans 10:10–11 says, "For with the heart man believeth unto righteousness; and with the mouth confession is made unto salvation. For the scripture saith, whosoever believeth on Him shall not be ashamed" (KJV).

Know this: The cure is Jesus, and it was not your fault. Repeat this: *It was not my fault.*

"…old things are passed away; behold and all things are become new" (2 Corinthians 5:17, KJV).

Prescription Three

The sexual abuse I suffered was not my fault and I forgive myself for self-afflicting myself with sorrow, pain, and abuse for what someone else did to me. Today, I am free from the bondage of the enemy.

This is a new day. No longer, blame yourself—it is not your fault. The responsibility lies with the adult; there are laws concerning this. It is unacceptable and inappropriate behavior. Even consensual sex with any child is prohibited thereby the laws of the land and God is violated.

Rape is unacceptable. If we look again to the story of David, we can draw several conclusions about why David did not properly address the issue. Could it be that he continued to convict himself of his sin with Bathsheba? Maybe he fell victim to the culture and treated his sons differently than his daughter, and therefore did not want to address his prince? Whatever the reason, when Amnon raped his sister Tamar, the crime of incest was punishable by death. David was angry; however, he did nothing to carry out the commandments of the law against Amnon, which later caused dissension and death within the family.

Transformation of the Mind

The mind is a powerful vehicle. It is characteristic of intellect and consciousness—a combination of perception, memory, emotion, will, and imagination. All of which can affect our beliefs and philosophy. Past events can also affect your ambition, your goals and vision. Typically, our environment shapes our thinking and either propels us forward or impels us backward. To transform our minds, we must change old methodologies and start anew—replacing the negative thoughts and memories with positive declarations.

Memory is not always negative. It also brings about change and success. We only remember a small percentage of what we hear or read. Whether you have short or long term memory, repetition can enhance your skills. I have mentioned several scriptures and have even taken the liberty to repeat a couple of the scripture verses and specific text throughout the chapters. I want to pull up defeat and replace it with win-win proclamations.

As we've read, Tarmar's abuse left her with tangled and complicated memories. To change her emotional state there needed to be a transformation of the mind.

Some look to drugs—pharmaceutics or narcotics. Nonetheless, it doesn't matter how many drugs you take; they will not erase the vivid images that flash before you from time to time. Even if you have commanded your memory not to produce flashbacks and have forced yourself not to remember the past, unless you have been healed by the power of Jesus, these memories will continue to torment you. They have a way of presenting themselves when all seems to be going well. They will also present themselves during transitional stages in life, such as the beginning of a marriage, the birth of your newborn, or the graduation of a son or daughter.

Smells and places can also trigger your memory to flash pictures of your past before you. My husband and I were walking in the parking lot of the shopping mall. We were holding hands and talking, and suddenly I knew someone smoking a cigar was in proximity—the smell whiffed by my nose. That was it for me. Pictures of the past flashed before me. My emotional state immediately changed. It took the wisdom of a man who stayed close to me through my healing process to encourage me and bring me back from this distress. I had just ridden an emotional rollercoaster.

Before my deliverance, I was an emotional nightmare for anyone who had to deal with me. In the beginning stages of my healing, I continually failed the test. Though I had someone to encourage me, *I* also had to cast down the images and my imagination and bring my mind into the mind of Christ. Transformation came when I decided that I no longer wanted to relive these epic scenes of torment. Now when the enemy tries his games, I can say with confidence, " … And cut! I am no longer available for "Showtime."

Philippians 2:5 tells us, "Let this mind be in you, which was also in Christ Jesus" (KJV). We can command our minds to line up with the Word of God. We don't have to beg, but we must command everything that is misaligned to line up with the mind and ways of Jesus.

2 Corinthians 5:17 says, "Therefore, if any man *be* in Christ, *he is* a new creature: old things are passed away; behold all things are become new" (KJV).

The AMP phrases that passage like this: "Therefore if any person is [ingrafted] in Christ (the Messiah) he is a new creation (a new creature together); the old [previous moral and spiritual condition] has passed away. Behold the fresh and new has come!"

The Word of God teaches us to be careful for nothing. In everything, by prayer and supplication and with thanksgiving, let our requests be known unto God. When we follow God's instructions, God promises us that the peace of God that shields us from worry keeps our hearts and minds in him. He also instructs us to only think, meditate, and fix our mind on these things:

- True things—eternal truth in creation and revelation

- Honest things—all that is honorable and decent to and before God

- Just things—justice, righteousness, and Christ-like

- Pure things—all that is holy
for body and soul

- Lovely things—all that is
pleasing and blesses others

- Things of good report—all that is
praiseworthy, of both public and private,
good report, as well as virtuous

(Philippians 4:8)

This is the antidote for our memories—it dis-avows the triggers for distress and pain. This is powerful! We don't have to suffer from torment-ing dreams, images, and memories. We can close the door and free ourselves from the power of the enemy. Jesus has redeemed us from the curse of the enemy. The strongholds of images and imaginations can now be brought into the obedience of Christ; we have the ability to cast them down. We have a weapon—it is the Word of God.

> (For the weapons of our warfare *are* not carnal, but mighty through God to the pulling down of strong holds;) Casting down imaginations, and every high thing that exalteth itself against the knowledge of God, and bringing into captivity every thought to the obedience of Christ.
>
> (2 Corinthians 10:4, KJV)

Here, Paul denies the charges of the false proph-ets, who had gained considerable ground by discred-iting him at Corinth. Though he lived in the flesh, he did not war after the flesh. His weapons were spiritual—he did not fight with human weaponry. We need weapons that are God-empowered to pull down anything opposing the will of God. Paul spoke specifically of warfare in the mind. If we bring into captivity every thought and turn it toward the obedience of Christ, we take every thought prisoner—flashbacks, dreams, and smells. Lascivious, vain, and evil thoughts of all kinds are brought down and made obedient to his laws. This includes any thinking, which is contrary to virtue, purity, and righteousness.

There are three great triumphs of spiritual warfare to help you close the door.

Destruction of Strongholds

We destroy dogmatic doctrines—the reasoning of pagan philosophers and false religions that nullify the Word of God and the facts of the gospel. We put to flight demon powers and alien armies who are designed to attack at the highest level.

Casting Down Imaginations

We demolish theories, the wisdom of this world, and any high system of ethics, religiosity, heathen worship, metaphysics, or philosophy set forth to defy the knowledge of God.

Bring Into Captivity

Every thought must turn to the obedience of Christ.
We take every vile evil, destructive thought, imagination, and dream captive into the obedience of
Christ. We stand in readiness offensively and defen-
sively to avenge all disobedience. Dressed with our
holy armor, we bring them down, and they are made
obedient to his laws.

Night Visions

When I was a little girl, I often experienced nightmares. Some were recurring. I was afraid to put my
feet on the floor; I thought the enemy would grab
my feet. I didn't want to look at the closet, because I
knew something was in it. Because there was demonic
activity in my house, these spirits took up residence
and were very much active in my house. My recurring dreams depicted me running from something
dark and unimaginable. I would often dream of
something being in my basement or coming through
the window. These dreams affected me into adulthood. I never wanted to go into any basement, and I
never wanted to be home by myself.

Though there are some misguided beliefs about
dreams, I know that my dreams were caused by major
conflict and traumatic experiences. In general, the
content of nightmares revolves around imminent
harm being caused to the individual having the nightmare, such as being chased, threatened, or injured,

for example. When nightmares occur as a part of post-traumatic stress disorder, or PTSD, they tend to involve the original threatening or horrifying set of circumstances involved during the traumatic event.

Author Thompson Gale, Detroit, Gale Encyclopedia of Childhood and Adolescent, 1998 writes that nightmares can begin at 18 month to 5 years of age. They can increase at the ages of three and six years old. Ten to fifty percent of these nightmares are considered serious enough to concern the parents. This does not mean that children with nightmares necessarily have psychological disorders. Typically, fifty percent of children who have not suffered traumatic events grow out of the nightmares as they get older. It is also reported that women tend to have more nightmares than men.

Statistics about these nightmares state that they generally cease once you become an adult, and this was true for me as well. Though the nightmares stopped as a child, I was succumbing to sexual incubus dreams as an adult. The dreams would occur periodically; I could never pinpoint why or when it was going to happen. They never involved people I knew, except the one time the enemy came to me in the form of my father. This spirit manifested itself and was revealed to my husband who was able to rebuke and eradicate the purpose and plot of this particular spirit.

One night, after flying home from my father's funeral in Georgia, I was tired. I went right to sleep without praying. Late that night, my husband was awakened by a foul odor.—A spirit had entered the room. At first, my husband didn't understand what was happening. He sat up in the bed and looked at me, only to realize I was sound asleep. The spirit began to manifest itself and speak. He asked my husband to let him have me. The spirit came in the form of my father. My husband rebuked it; he demanded it go back from whence it came and never come back again. The spirit began to plead, saying he was in hell and that he needed help. My husband took authority and let this spirit know it did not have legal rights over me; therefore, it had no right to present itself again. He evicted the spirit, commanding it never to return again. Thank God it was revealed—because of this, it has never returned.

Let's discuss the following scripture passage.

And it came to pass, that the beggar died, and was carried by the angels unto Abraham's bosom: the rich man also died and was also buried. And in hell he lifted his eyes, being in torments, and seeth Abraham afar off and Lazarus in his bosom. And he cried and said, Father Abraham, have mercy on me, and send Lazarus that he may dip the tip of his finger in water and cool my tongue; for I am tormented in this flame. But Abraham said, Son, remember that thou in thy lifetime receivest thy good things, and likewise Lazarus evil things: but now he is comforted, and thou art tormented. And beside all this, between us and you there is great gulf fixed: so that they which would pass from hence to you cannot; neither can they pass to us that *would* come from thence. Then he said, I pray thee therefore, father, that thou wouldest send him to my father's house. For I have five brethren; that he may testify unto them, lest they also come into this place of torment. Abraham saith unto him, They have Moses and the prophets: let them hear them. And he said, Nay father Abraham; but if one went unto them for the dead, they will repent. And he said unto him. If they hear not Moses and the prophets, neither will they be persuaded, though one rose from the dead.

(Luke 16:22–31, KJV)

Exegetically, I will address what the Bible says about heaven and hell. Without over literalizing, it is important to note that our focus should not be on the location of heaven or hell, but the dimension of both. In literal speech, heaven is a place where God dwells. It is eternal life, peace, joy, and happiness. Hell is a place of torment and loneliness. The greatest torment of hell is probably not being able to warn the living of such a place.

This scripture refers to a rich man and a beggar. Both lives were required of them. The beggar was carried into the bosom of Abraham, which is paradise. Jesus referred to this when he spoke to the thief on the cross. Before the resurrection of Christ, all righteous souls went to paradise, where they were held captive by the devil against their will. Christ went to the grave, then liberated the righteous, and took them with him when he ascended to heaven. Now, when the righteous die, they no longer go to the lower parts of the earth, but they immediately go to heaven in the resurrection of the body (2 Corinthian 5:6). Christ has the keys of Hades and of death and paradise, which are under the earth.

However, the tormented part of Hades continues to enlarge itself. It will hold all the wicked dead until the end of the millennium, when Hades will deliver up the souls in it. The graves will also give up their bodies and the souls, and the spirits of the wicked will be cast into the eternal hell (Revelation 20:11–15).

There is a gulf—Greek word *chasma*—a gaping opening whereby no one in heaven or hell can cross-over. This position cannot be changed; therefore, the dead cannot come back and visit us. Satan presented himself to my husband as my father. The spirit who represented my father said he was in hell; therefore, he could not crossover. These spirits are typically summoned by incantations, black magic, spells, and enchantments, though in my case, he wasn't.

I need to be clear; I wasn't there when my father passed away, so I have no idea whether he repented to God before or at the time of death. Therefore, it is not my call to say if the Lord received him in heaven, or if he now resides in hell. Nothing can be done if he is in hell because we cannot pray anyone into heaven, and there is no waiting place, or purgatory. If he is in heaven, glory be to God, who is the judge of us all.

The sexual dreams continued to occur. I later studied the incubus and succubus spirits and then realized what I was experiencing in my dreams. Without delay, I took authority over it and since then, I no longer have to battle with the incubus spirit.

The incubus and succubus spirit are two different spirits.

- A succubus is a demon who takes the form of a beautiful woman to seduce men in dreams by having sexual intercourse with them

- An incubus is a demon who comes in the form of a man to seduce a woman by having sexual intercourse with her in her dream. According to medieval European legend, the incubus would draw energy from the woman to sustain himself, often until the point of exhaustion of death of the victim

Demons even come in the form of hermaphrodites. Greek mythological character Hermaphroditus was the son of Hermes and Aphrodite and renowned for his beauty. A fountain nymph became enamored of him and asked the gods to unite her with him in one body. The result was a creature that was half man and half woman.

If you have experienced nightmares or seducing sexual spirits, don't worry—it is time for deliverance. We will take authority over these spirits in the next chapter.

CLOSE THE DOOR PART III—IT'S TIME TO WAR

Getting Connected— The Power of the believer

Every believer has the power to bring down the enemy's camp and declare victory for himself and his family. You have the power to be the victor and not the victim. What the enemy meant for evil, God turns into good, but these are just words if we don't believe them. Many times, we repeat scriptures or quotes that we have heard from others; these are just clichés and colloquialisms that have no power if we don't have understanding or knowledge of them. We must appreciate that God's Word is loaded with power. Satan would like to keep us ignorant to his kingdom, so for years we continue to pray amiss. In this mind-set, our prayers have no substance because we are entrenched with doubt, and Satan continues to gain ground. Doubt and worry are sins (Romans 14:23); they make us look away from God's promise and destiny and cause us to operate within our own intellect.

"What shall we say then? Shall we continue in sin, that grace may abound? God forbid, How shall we, that are dead to sin, live any longer therein? Know ye not, that so many of us as were baptized into Jesus Christ were baptized into his death? Therefore, we are buried with him by baptism into death: that like as Christ was raised up from the dead by the glory of the Father, even, so we also should walk in newness of life. For if we have been planted together in the likeness of his death, we shall be also *in the likeness* of *his* resurrection. Knowing this, that our old man is crucified with *him,* that the body of sin might be destroyed, that henceforth we should not serve sin. For he that is dead is freed from sin. Now if we be dead with Christ, we believe that we shall also live with him. Knowing that Christ being raised from the dead dieth no more; death hath no more dominion over him. For in that he died, he died unto sin once: but in that he liveth, he liveth unto God. Likewise reckon ye also yourselves to be dead indeed unto sin, but alive unto God through Jesus Christ our Lord. Let not sin therefore reign in your mortal body, that ye should obey it in the lusts thereof. Neither yield ye your members as instruments of unrighteousness unto sin: but yield yourselves unto God, as those that are alive from the dead, and your members as instruments of righteousness unto God. For sin shall not have dominion over you: for ye are not under the law, but under grace"

(Romans 6:1–14, KJV)

Romans 6:1–14 details the divine method of deliverance from sin, from which Satan wants to hold us captive. If we are in sin, then our prayers are hindered, and deliverance is just a word—it has no life or truth. Sin, rebellion, and disobedience open doors for curses, allowing Satan to have authority and cause affliction, calamity, and destruction. Once we are saved, we must be aware of the devil's devices. We cannot be entangled with his yoke of bondage. We cannot return to bondage, we cannot touch the unclean thing. We must repent of all sins, and we must live a life that is holy before God so that our prayers are not amiss. We must also submit our will to God's will (Matthew 6:10). This releases the power of God upon us and connects us to his plan.

To begin, we will clothe ourselves with the armor of God (Ephesians 6:11). This scripture is a promise and a command made so that we may be able to stand against the wiles of the devil. Wiles are the methods used to entrap and enslave the souls of man. The enemy thrust fiery darts, Greek word *belos* toward his target. To describe the darts we could call them missiles or combustible arrows—used to penetrate through the shield and armor. These spears, or combustible arrows, are designed to attack your faith, emotion, finance, family, church, home, and job. They are lusts, evil thoughts, passions, and temptation of various kinds. This is why the shield, helmet and breastplate are needed.

The Believers' Armor

The Lord warns and admonishes us to put on the *whole* armor of God. Having the cloak of armor makes you invulnerable and victorious. Every saint, every believer should clothe themselves in the armor. It is a spiritual mind-set to be ready to do battle. Let us examine the armor.

Ephesians 6:13 says, "Wherefore take unto you the whole armor of God that ye may be able to withstand in the evil day, and having done all, to stand" (KJV).

In the AMP, the same verse says, "Therefore put on God's complete armor, that you may be able to resist *and* stand your ground on the evil day [of danger], and, having done all [the crises demands], to stand [firmly in your place]."

The helmet—Greek translation *perikephalaia*— the helmet of a Roman soldier was made of iron, bronze and other sturdy material. The high priest had a golden plate on the front of his vesture that said "Holy to the LORD." The helmet figuratively refers to salvation, or the protection of your soul. Salvation is a present experience of the Lord's deliverance of believers who have battled the spiritual conflict of this world. If worn daily, it will renew our minds daily—keeping us in the right mind, with right thinking, and it will be a part of the salvation process. It keeps us emotionally sound. The mind is the battlefield; the helmet helps us to hear the voice of God and to see into the spirit realm. Thus, we are not moved by what our natural ears hear and what our natural eyes see.

The girdle—Greek word *zoma*—A protective apron that fits tightly around the body, holding the daggers, swords and other instruments. It is a thick leather belt fastened for readiness and active service for the Lord. It is the sash of truth that keeps us from living a life of deception. It keeps our lips from lying, which allows us to serve God in spirit and in truth; this allows deliverance in our lives.

Truth

The breastplate—Greek translations *thorax*—is a corselet consisting of two parts. It protects the body on both sides, from the neck to the middle. It extends down to the legs. This protects our vital organs—our righteousness, faith, and love by keeping our heart toward God. It keeps us in right standing with the Father. As it says in Job 29:14, "I put on righteousness, and it clothed me" (KJV). The breastplate allows us to be synchronized to the will of God—not our will, but thy will, will be done.

Hearts towards God ↓ God's will

The brazen boots—Greek translation *knemides*—covers part of the leg and protects the feet from thorns and stones. The boots keep us on a sure foundation. Our feet are shod with the preparation of the gospel of peace; allowing us to excel with peace in

Foundation

peace.

every battle or storm. They enable tranquility, harmony, and peace between individuals.

The shield—Greek translation *tureos*—is large and oblong. The shield protects every part of the body from blows and cuts. It is a repellent for fiery darts and daggers from the enemy. It is our shield of faith that protects the religious beliefs of Christians—the fidelity and faithfulness. It protects a strong conviction that Jesus is the Messiah through whom we obtain salvation in the kingdom of God. We have to live with the shield. "The just shall live by faith" (Romans 1:17 KJV).

The sword—Greek translation *macgaura*—is the Word of God. It destroys the enemy and brings submission to the power of God.

Girding ourselves daily is a command from God. It ensures we are prepared. The readiness of the armor repels the enemy. His darts are to cause doubt, shame, and no forgiveness. With confidence, we walk in unshakable and remarkable faith. We are free from doubt so that we are not tossed back and forth like the waves. We are rooted and grounded in truth—no more carried about by every wind or doctrine. The helmet and sash allow us freedom from deception and illusions so we can discern error and speak truth in love.

Each part of the armor works together with the others. From the crowns of our heads to soles of our feet, we must be covered. Now that we understand the concept and importance of the armor, let us move forward to discuss the kingdom of Satan.

Ephesians 6:18 commands us to, "Pray at all times (on every occasion, in every season) in the Spirit, with all [manner of] prayer and entreaty. To that end, keep alert and watch with strong purpose and perseverance, interceding in behalf of all the saints (God's consecrated people)" (AMP).

This is a scripture of command—always pray in the spirit, in every appeal and petition. We don't want to stop at the armor; we will need to incorporate prayer as well. Prayer is needed in addition to the armor and very important to fight against spiritual powers of evil. Some put on the chief outfit, but never avail against the hostile onslaughts.

Understanding Satan's Kingdom

Satan has an organized kingdom—a strategic army. Having usurped man's dominion, he is the ruler of the air of this world. Satan with his trusted angels—demons and imps, they are responsible for carrying out his will over the governments of this world. He seeks to hinder God's plan for the fulfillment of prophecy, regarding world kingdoms. Additionally, there are good and evil spiritual beings seeking to influence and carry out the will of their masters. We must pray strategically. It is amazing what we will see if we seek to go past the natural. The enemy has gained momentum because many do not take prayer seriously. Knee time in the spirit will bring about change. It is in the spirit realm that we understand our opponent's passion and strategy. Learning what we are dealing with enables us strategic movement to break the bands of the enemy. Out of tradition, I thought I knew how to intercede in the spirit. I didn't gain knowledge of the strategic steps and preparation for warfare until after seeking God and studying the Word of God.

Ephesians 6:12 (KJV) says, "For we wrestle not against flesh and blood but against principalities, against powers, against rulers of the darkness of this world, against spiritual wickedness in high *places.*"

The Greek word for wrestle is *pale,* but here, it refers to warfare in general between saints and rebel spirits. Let us examine the spirits of rebels.

In my study, it became clear that each power is representative of specific strongholds—demons, devils, and evil spirits. I learned that when I pray for governmental systems and education, I must target principalities. I would target the powers of evil spirits and bind them concerning the possibility of freak accidents. Lets' look at these a little closer.

Principalities, or Greek word *arche,* mean the beginning, or origin. Principalities denotes the first position and order of angels, supreme powers or chief rulers or being of the highest rank and order in Satan's kingdom. This ruling power usually attacks world leaders. They are evil angels, ruling the kingdoms of the world that oppose the truth of God and of which Satan is the chief prince or ruler. Remember, these angels had authoritative power assigned to them by God, which they left, aspiring to prohibited conditions. Now they report to Satan and operate to oppose the truth of God.

In Matthew 12:24, the devil is called "Beelzebub," meaning lord of the dwelling in which these wicked spirits are subjects. They—like their chief prince—direct, control, rule, and carry out the present darkness of this world.

Powers, or Greek word *exousias,* means authority, influence, and of right privilege. They are the next in the chain of angels who operate in high places, who derive their power from and execute the will of chief rulers. These are universal powers that rule and govern. They are powers of judicial decisions over jurisdictions. This would include all high-ranking, evil, supernatural powers, and the power of sin and evil in operation in the world. Their assignments are delegated from principalities. They attach and infect structures of government, and the five pillars of society: marriage, family, government, education, and church (Colossians 2:15; Ezekiel 28:1–10). The fruits of this type of evil can be seen in drug cartels, gross poverty, plagues, terrorism, and other heinous crimes against humanity, even toward the animal kingdom.

The Greek word *kosmkratoras skotois toutou* means "the ruler of darkness of this world." The lord of the world—the prince of this age is the devil, along with his demons. The phrase "ruler of the darkness" refers both to humans and to the angel of death. Their mission is to try and interrupt time and space, refute the existence of God, and convince man to believe in science. They are responsible for blinding the spiritual and moral senses by binding the minds of people, which causes spiritual darkness and depravity of thoughts, feelings, and perceptions. The vehicles by which they operate are mass media, music, movies, fashion, sports, philosophies, and religious ideologies (Colossians 1:13; Revelation 16:10; Jude 1:6).

Pneumatika ponéria epouranios translates to "spiritual wickedness in heavenly places." These are wicked spirits of Satan working through countless agents mentioned in Ephesians 6:12. In this verse Paul the writer, is talking about cosmic warfare. Ponéria means the heavenly realm epouranios—its emphases are on the evil of spiritual control and forces against which we struggle. Responsible for depravity or malice; it denotes a vicious disposition, which is debased, warped, or corrupt, particularly in the sense of lewdness, malice, mischief, sin, and iniquity. They are additionally responsible for influencing and seducing, and also responsible for affecting motivation, fantasy, and imagination. They affect the appetite through overt or covert attack and influence of the mind, affecting the terrestrial and celestial domains. Their purpose is to hinder the believer's prayers. While you are praying, they have already sent out agents that will try and bind the prayer before it reaches the third heaven. They operate in the second heaven, Daniel 10:10–13 can be used as an example. An angel—a messenger from God was sent to David to advise of the unveiling blessing and information concerning the secrets of Persia; however, the Prince of the kingdom Persia withstood—

blocked the pathway for twenty-one days. Michael the chief princes came as reinforcement to help and clear the pathway. This reveals that a heavenly war occurred—a conflict between God and Satan. These are heavenly and satanic forces.

Greek word *daimonion* means devils and demons. The word "demon" is not found in scripture, but it means evil spirits or devil. Satan is the chief devil. Acts 17:18; it denotes an inferior pagan deity. "Demons" are the spiritual agent acting as idolatry. Satan is the prince of the devils and has an angelic body. He cannot enter bodily into anyone, though demons are disembodied spirits. They are evil spirits, or the messengers and ministers of the devil, responsible for a host of diabolical activities. They have the ability to distribute fortune. These spirits, like others, look for a live host; they can then possess man and control mind-sets and activities. Devils are worshiped. Additionally, they can make people sick. Evil spirits or *Ponéria* causes calamities. They are vicious and malicious spirits that work with other spirits that report directly to Satan. They are responsible for bad nature and conditions, as well as accidents, mishaps, and criminal activity. (See principalities—Luke 7:21) Unclean spirits, or *akathartos*, are spirits that are responsible for lewd, promiscuous, and unnatural affection. They desensitize the moral thinking, producing immoral activities (Mark 1:27).

Owb, or familiar spirits, implies the spirit of a dead one. A necromancer is one who evokes the dead. Familiar spirits can also be secret agents assigned to you by Satan. They take note of your shortcomings and other activities. Any doubt that you may speak into the atmosphere, they report back to the enemy's camp (Leviticus 20:6).

Now that we have examined the powers of wickedness, we will focus on wickedness in high places. These powers come to influence many with unnatural affection—homosexual and lesbian appetites—and perversions. They bind and enslave many with pornography and crimes.

To every believer and intercessor: once you know what you are dealing with, you can be equipped for war. Demons recognize the power of the believer, and they fear the power of God in the believer. They know the intercessor's name and are subject to the power of the intercessor. Their purpose is to wage war on the believer. Our armor is prayer and the armor of God.

Many do not believe that prayer is the key. We are living in a different time. God is a progressive God and is always moving. As the world has progressed, so has God. As sin abounds, grace did abound much more. Our God is always on the move. This is why the church must always progress and move with the times. Hence, we cannot pray antiquated and historical prayers; our grandmothers prayed for the rent, housing, food, etc. These needs are already taken care of. These issues are guaranteed favorable if we believe. The enemy's mission is to consume us with issues that the Lord has already taken care of. Exhausted, we lose focus and never war for family or the kingdom. We cannot lose focus—it is wartime.

Too often the TV, computer, and affairs of this world consume us, and prayer is no longer a priority or way of life. We have heard that these are the end-times. Christians must pray to endure: to hold our ground in conflict, bear up against adversity, hold out under stress, stand firm, preserve under pressure, and wait calmly and courageously. Matthew 24:13 tells us to endure to the end that we shall be saved. As we go on with our day-to-day lives, we don't want to be caught sleepwalking. This resembles a zombie—no power and no life—no dreams and no goals, and utterly overwhelmed with depression. I find that some Christians today don't fast as our spiritual parents fasted. We don't find ways to commune with God anymore. I remember going on absolute fasts—not eating anything for a few days—or a partial fast, which included only one meal at 5:00 p.m. for days. This also meant no television and no phone calls. These prayers and fasts elicited results; people were delivered and healed. If we want to see the power of God, we have to spend time with God. Why? Our young are being attacked on a greater level than when we were young adults. Our little children are succumbing to freak accidents and evil spirits. Parents are burying their children—this is not normal.

Children are also succumbing to unnatural affection. Today, unclean spirits have taken authority in regions. This spirit cannot just be cast out of the person but out of the region. It has become common practice for women to have sexual relationships with women and men to have sexual relationships with men.

This spirit also goes undercover. There are men that play-act and dress masculine to cover up their homosexual tendencies. Additionally, husband and wives, unbeknownst to each other, are involved in homosexual and lesbian relationships outside of the marriage. One morning I rode through a Park and Ride commuter lot in my area. The men that were picking up other men astonished me. Business men—college students—married men, some with baby car seats, all meeting to engage in romance and sexual orientation.

When I was younger, I dealt with this familiar spirit. Though I fought off women who wanted to be with me as a teenager, the satanic attack is greater for my children. Sexual perversion is no longer just on the TV and computer; now, children have iPods and Blackberry phones and can receive sexual e-mails and text messages. Sex has hit the airwaves and cyberspace. Therefore, we must study how to pray strategically—to know what to attack when we pray.

Knowing the structure of Satan's kingdom will help us to understand each battalion. Soldiers, boxers, and athletes learn their opponents. Before they go into the ring or the field, they study their strengths, tactics, strategies, and weaknesses. Many Christians are anxious to cast a demon out without learning the demon. If we would study the demons and their diabolical alliances and effects, we would always recognize the enemy, regardless of time or place. We could then see that behind different faces are the same demons.

When we pray, we pray in heavenly places, attacking cyberspace, the celestial and terrestrial, and pray against every catastrophic wind.

Ephesians 1:3 tells us, "Blessed be the God and Father of our Lord Jesus Christ, who hath blessed us with all spiritual blessings in heavenly places in Christ:" (KJV).

The Greek translation for heavenly places is *eulogia,* or blessings, which pertains to heaven and the celestial.

While we are deliberating the enemy's kingdom, let us look at key factors that will hinder prayers and prevent us from hitting our targets.

- Not Holy before God
- Praying amiss
- Not praying in the Holy Spirit
- Praying worries, problems and in emotions
- Not praying the Word of God
- Praying without believing

No matter the fervency of the prayer, if we don't have the first commandment—love—and have not humbled ourselves, or if there is no submission to God, our prayers will not be answered.

2 Chronicles 7:14 makes it clear that we have to turn from our wicked ways and seek His face; then we will hear from heaven, and God will heal us. When we revere God, we can move into our kingly anointing.

Kingly and Priestly Anointing

We have a kingly and priestly anointing; however, most saints only operate in their priestly anointing, which is called praise. This anointing points to reconciliation, intercession and worship. We all know how to praise God, sing unto God, and some of us can even worship God. Unfortunately, we are not clear about our kingly anointing; the kingly anointing refers to government, dominion, and authority. This anointing releases power to legislate, constitute, regulate, and rule. When we make declarations in faith we are operating in the kingly anointing. David's relationship with God and his leadership aptitude demonstrate the kingly and priestly anointing at work. He not only was a king but he was a true worshiper, who desired to be in the presence of God and communion with God. The kingly and priestly anointing is essential. When they work in accord it is the culmination—from praise and worship to proclamation and declaration. Hence, we are no longer praying our worries and concerns, but we have tapped into the heavenly place to legislate. The posture of a king is to reign, rule, legislate, and constitute.

For example: *Yes, I was molested; however, I praise you, Lord, because you are the God of an expected end. You are Jehovah Rophe, my healer. You are my refuge and deliverance. I worship you for your sovereignty. Thank*

you Lord; I am free, and every diabolical force that has attached itself to me must be bound and loosed today. I decree my mind is free, and I walk in the liberty of Christ. I am above and not beneath. Hallelujah!

Notice that I am not complaining about what happened. I no longer need to figure it out; God's unadulterated and irrefutable word has revealed the enemy and his plot. Now I praise, worship, and proclaim my victory. It is important to pray above principalities, in heavenly places, or spiritual wickedness will prohibit and frustrate your prayers. Our prayer must be directed by the Holy Spirit, and not by our emotions. This is hitting your target.

We can then pray against principalities that have attacked the government and the rulers of darkness who have attacked our children. The Word of God tells us that the spirit knows what to pray (Romans 8:26). This refers to the Holy Spirit. It reveals the secret things; everything that is hidden has the ability to become known in prayer. You are also part of the strategy—strategically placed in the kingdom to war for those who are captive to the devil.

I have witnessed many in our ministry and other ministries being delivered from the power of darkness. My husband once preached out of town at a deliverance service. Praise and worship were high, and many were being delivered during the worship.

There was a woman who was kneeling on the floor, holding her head, and calling out, "Stop, stop!" She then began to bang her head on the wall. I noticed what was happening and asked for assistance to pick her up and take her out of the service to pray for her. Once we were out, I knew this deliverance could not have happened in the sanctuary. She began to vomit blood and cry. She pretended she was delivered, but we knew she wasn't. We took authority over the enemy by binding the powers of darkness that night, and she was delivered. The next morning, she came to the fellowship breakfast and gave her testimony in front of everyone. She said that she was invited to the evening service, and that she didn't plan on attending. Instead, she decided to come, and once the service was over, she was going home to take her life. We thank God that the Lord intervened and delivered that woman.

Establish Your Rights

So many Christians are never delivered from bondage. They struggle with strongholds and demonic forces their entire Christian walk. Sometimes, it is because they refuse to live a life of holiness and, thus, lack the power. Other times, they are not taught or trained to use their God-given authority. They constantly go before God and plead with him to help them, when God has already said he has given us power and authority over the enemy. Today, we can establish our legal rights and walk in the authority of Jesus Christ.

People come to church for different reasons. Some come to network, others come to find a husband or wife, and some come to socialize. Not everyone comes to worship. Our noonday service is different than Sunday or our weekly prayer. It is not the pastors or co-laborers that have summoned these people to come—they come because they want a relationship with God. These prayers are at another level. Most everyone coming is coming with expectation, which activates the supernatural. Many come and receive the Holy Spirit. I have even seen deliverance for some who were struggling with the powers of darkness for years. Legal rights are established in these prayers. The powers of darkness have no other choice but to submit to the power of God.

What are your legal rights?

- Use of the name of Jesus
- Power to bind the strongman and subordinate spirits
- Power to resist the devil, and he will flee
- Use of the Word of God
    - Close the door and establish God as the new gatekeeper
    - Bind the work of the enemy and make it a part of Jesus' footstool (1 John 3:8)

- Loose every sign, condition, and
  effect associated with the enemy
- The believer has power to
  bind and to loose

"Verily I say unto you, whatsoever ye shall bind on earth shall be bound in heaven: and whatsoever ye shall loose on earth shall be loosed in heaven" (Matthew 18:18, KJV).

Deo, or "to bind," means to fasten with chains, or to put under obligation of the law. A binding takes place the earthly realm. God cosigns it and it is thereby bound in the heavenly realm. It is a restraining order that puts a restraint on the activity of the enemy—the Word of God and the blood of Jesus binds them.

Lyo, or "to loose," means to dissolve the spirit into two parts, or to overthrow the spirit, thereby demolishing and destroying the effects of the enemy. It is the opposite of binding. When Jesus healed and delivered, the symptoms giving evidence were loosed from whomever he healed. The effects of the enemy were destroyed; the strong man was gone, and the healed were loosed from the infirmity.

> "Now Jesus was teaching in one of the synagogues on the Sabbath. And there was a woman there who for eighteen years had an infirmity caused by a spirit (a demon of sickness). She was bent completely forward and utterly unable to straighten herself up *or* to look upward. And when Jesus saw her, He called [her to Him] and said to her,

Woman you are released from your infirmity! Then He laid [His] hands on her, and instantly she was made straight, and she recognized *and* thanked *and* praised God."

(Luke 13:10–13, AMP)

In the King James Version, verse twelve says, "Woman, thou art loosed from thine infirmity."

Binding and loosing work together by superimposing a new set of orders. To superimpose means to place over, overlay, apply to, or cover up. Therefore, we place the blood of Jesus—the spoken word of faith, healing, and deliverance—on the person, place, or thing. This leads me to talk about the victim's deliverance. Many who have been abused, though afraid to talk about it, are in need of deliverance from the same spirit. It may come in another form, but it is still the work of the enemy.

Often, those who were sexually abused are bound for years with spirits such as:

Incest	Pornography	Fornication
Adultery	Homosexuality	Lesbianism
Masturbation	Sexual orgies	Sexual fantasies and lust
Nightmares from incubus and succubus spirits		

It is interesting that although most of these are often talked about in our churches, masturbation is rarely talked about among the women in ministry.

However, questions are asked concerning masturbation: *Is it a sin? Is it healthy? Is dry sex and sex without penetration acceptable?* Allow me to delineate. Masturbation is an erotic stimulation of one's own genital organs commonly resulting in orgasm and achieved by manual or other bodily contact exclusive of sexual intercourse, by instrumental manipulation, occasionally by sexual fantasies, or by various combinations of these agencies, which are called *self-abuse.* The term *Onanism,* derived from Genesis 38:9; it is often referred to as masturbation. The scripture says that when Onan cohabited with his brother's widow, he spilled the seed to the ground and prevented conception. In no way, does this prove masturbation on Onan's part—but illustrates coitus interruptus-the deliberate withdraw and avoidance of ejaculation, which is a method of birth control.

Having no clue of the spiritual ramifications, many Christian leaders mislead parishioners concerning this topic; thereby, giving way for strongholds and spirits to hold its victim captive. These doors are hard to close without prayer and fasting.

Masturbation is a subordinate spirit that controls the mind. Most in general, imagination is necessary or active to obtain an orgasm. Some women imagine a man, women, or both in conjunction with them during the sexual encounter. Many have gone to great extremes to encounter the desired climax. This is why sex toys are used. If sex toys are not available, this spirit controls the mind and suggests other objects—oblong fruit—vegetables—bottles—vibrators—showerheads to be used as an aide to pleasure. And often times, infections are caused by using such instruments.

The enemy's secret must be unveiled concerning this spirit. It is a stronghold that refuses to loose its hold off the women of God. It is flesh warring against the spirit. When you think you are done and free from this spirit, it refuses to divorce you, and draws you back in by means of TV—video—music and loneliness. It takes the power of God to command it to loose its claws and let you go. The Bible says in 2 Corinthians 10:3–5 (KJV), "For though we walk in the flesh, we do not war after the flesh: (For the weapons of our warfare are not carnal, but mighty through God to the pulling down of strong holds); Casting down imaginations, and every high thing that exalteth itself against the knowledge of God, and bringing into captivity every thought to the obedience of Christ."

To ensure the three questions that have been posed in the beginning of the topic are answered, I will conclude with the sin that masturbation falls under. Masturbation is one of the sexual immoralities that falls under fornication. When one masturbates they sin against their own body. The scriptures lets us know that our body is not our own to do what we please, but we have been bought with a price. Let's look at what the writer Paul has to say about this.

> "Flee fornication. Every sin that a man doeth is without the body; but he that committeth fornication sinneth against his own body. What? Know ye not that your body is the temple of the

Holy Ghost which is in you, which ye have of God, and ye are not your own?"

(1 Corinthians 6:18–19 KJV)

The Amplified says it like this.

"Shun immorality *and* all sexual looseness [flee from impurity in thought, word, or deed]. Any other sin which a man commits is one outside the body, but he who commits sexual immorality sin against his own body. Do you not know that your body is the temple (the very sanctuary) of the Holy Spirit Who lies within you, Whom you have received [as a Gift] from God? You are not your own"(1 Corinthians 6:18–19, AMP).

The sash—the believer's armor of God—has to be wrapped closely around the loins so that we do not deceive ourselves. Trust will make the devil a liar, and deliverance will burst forward. Every unclean spirit will then have to loose its hold and take flight, because it can no longer be housed in a vessel that has denounced it.

Before we move on to the next chapter, I believe it is fitting to discuss the power of touching and agreeing. I want to cover this, because there are spirits from whom I believe God wants his people delivered.

The Power of Touching and Agreeing

When we touch and agree, or "hook up" with someone in the spirit realm, it unleashes the supernatural power. Definitively, it will be done—prayers are answered. The key here is to hook up and be in harmony with the other participant. If the other participant is not in harmony with you during the prayer, the prayer is null and void. If they lack faith, the prayer is hindered.

Today I want to touch and agree with you to take authority over spirits who have invaded your being. I take authority over these spirits, who feel they have rights over you, and bind them in the name of Jesus. I loose every effect of wickedness in high places, rulers of darkness, powers of this world, and evil spirits. Today, I decree that the unclean spirit who has invaded your life must be released. You are set free from the power of the enemy, and these acts and addictions no longer hold you captive.

This is your assignment: Call out the name of the attack, the assignment of the enemy, and denounce Satan. Let him know he no longer has authority or power over you.

Let's seal this declaration with prayer.

God, in the name of Jesus, I am free of the attack of the enemy. I am covered in your blood; therefore, the enemy cannot enter. His plots and ploys have been returned to the sender. Lord, you said that no weapon formed against me shall prosper. Today, God, I stand on your Word. Father, you said if I pray and believe it shall be done. Let kingdom come today. Lord, I praise you for victory. In Jesus' name.

Matthew 18:19–20 (KJV) says, "Again I say unto you, That if two of you shall agree on earth as touching anything that they shall ask, it shall be done for them of my Father which is in heaven. For where two or three are gathered together in my name, there am I in the midst of them".

"Again" also means "assuredly." It applies to prayer in general, but more specifically, it concerns the divine guidance that is sought and received in matters of discipline, to guard against dissensions and schisms (1 Corinthians 1:10).

Sumphoneo—sum, "together;" and *phoneo*, "to sound"—means to agree, to sound together, to be in accord, and to be in harmony. Metaphorically, the word means in concordant to agree together in prayer.

When we come together and agree, we then constitute the omnipresence of Christ—his presence is in our midst. God is in our midst—he is the omnipresence, omniscience, and omnipotence of Christ among the believers. In concordance with another believer—in one mind, we are in the omnipresence of Christ.

In the Psalm 110:1–2 (KJV), the Lord of the universe told David's Lord to rejoice; to "sit at the right hand, Till I make your enemies Your footstool." He went on to say, "The Lord shall send the rod of thy strength out of Zion: rule thou in the mist of thine enemies." This was a prophecy.

The Lord, the Creator of this universe is touching and agreeing with the Messiah in the spirit realm. This is the Holy Spirit in fullness. To understand the scripture, we must understand that Jehovah spoke to Jehovah. The Lord, the Messiah, is God in the flesh. Here, God agreed with himself—one accord and one mind. God made covenant with himself when he created the universe.

When we agree, not only do we agree with the other person praying with us, but also we must agree with God—His Word and His will. When we don't have anyone to agree with us, we can agree with our Creator and our Lord, the Father, the Son, and the Holy Spirit. We settle our prayer in heaven and on earth. Hallelujah! This is agreeing power!

Let's look to another healing prescription.

Prescription Four

I clothe myself with the whole armor of God, and I superimpose the blood of Jesus and the plan of God over principalities, powers, and rulers of darkness of this world, spiritual wickedness in high places, demons, the devil, and evil spirits concerning every area of my life. The enemy has become a part of Jesus footstool and I have nothing to worry about.

Here is a prayer of deliverance.

I praise you for your son Jesus Christ, who came and took our sins, and we took on Calvary's power. First, I am in covenant with you; second, I have been redeemed from sickness, poverty and the curse of the law. Therefore, I bind spiritual wickedness in high places that attack my senses, thoughts, and imaginations. I loose the effects of incest, molestation, and rape. Whatsoever is bound and loosed on earth is bound and loosed in heaven, for my God cosigns it in heaven. I superimpose the effects of the enemy by placing the blood of Jesus that heals and delivers. I break all soul ties that have come as a spiritual decoy, and I sever them in the spirit realm. I take authority over every unclean spirit, principalities, and evil spirits. Their plots and ploys are returned to dry places. Lord, release the angelic host and intercessor to war on my behalf; let them not come down from their watchtowers until their assignments are done.

I decree that there is a turnaround. I roam where the kings roam. Every seductive and influential spirit is broken and no longer holds me captive. I declare I am free from shame. The blood of Jesus destroys the gripping hold of mental anguish, control, sexual addictions, nightmares, and fetish behaviors today.

I proclaim wholeness today. I walk in the promises of the Lord. This prayer hits the target, and I speak to the atmosphere, stratosphere, hemisphere, and I settled it in the earth realm in Jesus' name.

GIVE ME BACK MY PEARLS

A pearl is developed through irritation. It is formed when some small object, typically a parasite or piece of organic matter, becomes embedded in the tissue of an oyster or mollusk. As a result, the mantle tissue of the mollusk secretes *nacre,* also known as the mother of pearl. Chemically speaking, this is calcium carbonate and a fibrous protein called *conchiolin.* As the *nacre* builds in layers, it surrounds the irritant and eventually forms a pearl.

Looking for Something Called Love

There is a myth about the grain of sand—that the irritant develops the pearl. A grain of sand is gritty, coarse, and rough. Clearly, this is what my life was before my pearl was fully developed. My life was rough; I sold out to drugs as an escape. I was a functional addict. I went to work every day and lived a granular life that forced me to play out an illusion—a woman who had it all together. My marriage, for the first ten years, was bumpy—enmeshed with insecurity, instability, and sexual enslavement. I couldn't be a wife or mother because I didn't know how. I was never privy to a father who loved his wife like Christ loved the church, or a father who was the protector of his girls. I don't remember the hugs and natural kisses of a husband and wife or father and daughter from growing up.

Moreover, once I finished high school, I fled to find refuge. I was in pursuit of love outside of my house. I am reminded of the story of Dinah. She lived in a dysfunctional family and later went looking for the daughters in the land. She found a man named Shechem, who fell in love with her. That is not how it actually happened. Shechem manipulated and beguiled Dinah, then defiled her. After the act his soul, the seat of his emotions desired her, and he fell in love with her (Genesis 35:1–3).

The name Dinah means, "Vindicated," suggesting that Leah believed God was vindicating her in her struggle with Rachel over the affections of Jacob. Dinah came from a family of drama. Her mother Leah was given to Jacob out of deception. However, Jacob loved Rachel; he worked for fourteen years to have her as his wife. His boss was Laban, Leah and Rachel's father. The Word of God says that Jacob loved Rachel more than he did Leah. Leah was the woman Jacob married, but Rachel was the woman

Jacob loved. Leah had seven of his babies, she was married to him, but he never loved her. In contrast, and because Rachel was barren, she hated Leah. God knew it, and that is why he opened Leah's womb.

Leah conceived and bore a son, and she called him Reuben. She thought that surely, the Lord had looked upon her affliction; therefore, Jacob would love her—but he didn't. She conceived and bore Simeon, and she said it was because the Lord heard that she was hated. Leah conceived and bore Levi. Leah believed that Jacob would then be joined unto her, but she was wrong. She conceived and bore Judah and said that then she would praise the Lord.

When Rachel saw Leah's blessings and knew she still could not have children, she envied Leah and asked Jacob to give her children, or she would die. Jacob granted her wish and Rachel had a couple of children through her maid. Whose names are Bilhas, which means—"God hath judge me and heard my voice," and Naphtali whose name means "with great wrestling has she wrestled with her sister and she have prevailed."

At this time Leah could not bear, so she took her maid Zilpah to Jacob to bear another son—Gad, meaning "a troop cometh." She also gave birth to another son, Asher, meaning "happiness or blessedness."

And the story goes on to say that around this time, Reuben, Leah's son, found some mandrakes— a lettuce-like plant of dark green color with purple flowers and fruit about the size of a small apple. Used as a love potion, it would induce conception by eating. Rachel pleaded for Leah's son to give her some of the mandrakes. Verses 15–16 lets us know what Leah's response was:

> "But [Leah] answered, Is it not enough that you have taken my husband without taking away my son's mandrakes also? And Rachel said, Jacob shall sleep with you tonight [in exchange] for your son's mandrakes. And Jacob came out of the field in the evening, and Leah went out to meet him and said, You must sleep with me [tonight], for I have certainly paid your hire with my son's mandrakes. So he slept with her that night."
>
> (Genesis 30:15–16, AMP)

Rachel had faith in superstition and agreed to let Leah have Jacob for the mandrakes as payment for a night of romance. The Bible says that God hearkened unto Leah, and she conceived another son, Issachar. Leah now thought the women would call her happy and blessed and think that God had given her hire. She had a sixth son, Zebulun. God had endowed her, and she thought then her husband would dwell with her, but he didn't.

Leah then conceived her seventh child, and she thought this was it—her seventh child, the number of perfection. She bore Dinah. However, no meaning and no purpose were given. Children were regarded as a special gift from God, but males especially were very important to build and preserve the family.

This story depicts a woman named Leah who desperately thought that after she had given birth to each child, Jacob would intimately be drawn closer to her, and that he would love her more. Nonetheless, Jacob's heart was still toward Rachel and this left Leah embittered and frustrated.

For years, Leah and Rachel feuded over Jacob for love and legacy. Dinah grew up witnessing the feud, and this explains why Dinah went looking for women—she was looking for friendship and love outside of the house. Instead, she met a man who showed her what she never received or witnessed at home. Though Shechem—the son of Hamor the Hivite, prince of the country—lay with her and defiled her, he tried to make it right. He told her father that he had to have her as his wife. To make it right, he offered pieces of silver (Genesis 30: 1–21).

Women today who are hurt and abused are still looking for love in people and things. I have spiritually counseled many women, and they are consumed with emotion: living with men who will not marry them, will not serve God, or treat them as the pearls they are. In this day, there are still women who are having babies to secure relationships with men.

My sisters, babies will not keep him. A man cannot be put in a box. If he feels restraints, he will run. He will hide, especially if he is not ready for responsibility. Maybe he never had a good example of family or a father. Sometimes, we watch too many movies or soap operas and try to scheme and plan a way to keep a man. If he doesn't love you, he can't be kept.

You must know that you are a pearl; do not give your pearls to swine—there are those who have no idea of the value and beauty of the pearl. Irritation of the oyster—your past—has developed you into who you are today, and anyone who refuses to examine the pearl to see the beauty does not have the ability to hold the pearl with care. If it is placed in the wrong hands, with ignorance, they will throw it away. If they don't immediately throw it away, they are parasites—leeches, freeloaders, and sponges who do not care. They only came to use you up and then throw you away as damaged goods.

Women who are abused are often called "damaged goods," and can usually be spotted by those who prey on women. If you have not healed, then the last thing you need at this time is a relationship. You first must be healed, or you are bringing your baggage with you.

When a man loves you, he holds the pearl (you), he examines its worth and beauty (that cannot be purchased by man) and he cherishes and protects it—it is then sealed in the palm of his hand.

I mentioned damaged goods in this book a couple of times. Damage goods—speckled prey has value. If you read the story of Jacob, you can better understand the meaning of "speckled prey." Genesis 30:32–43 tells us that speckled and spotted animals were rare. Jacob wanted a new starting point with Laban—a boss who was unjust, covetous, and shameful. Laban was a boss and father-in-law who deceived Jacob, changing his wages ten times.

Here we see two manipulators come together. Laban tries to manipulate the manipulator—Jacob, but fails. It is interesting that God allowed Laban to come into Jacob's life only to remove the characteristic of a trickster and conman. Laban—a manipulator—not wanting to lose Jacob says. "Name me your wages and I will give." Jacob—the swindler wanted to go and provide for his own house. Laban took everything that he earned, and prohibited Jacob from establishing his own household. Consequently, Jacob did not want Laban to give him anything, but agreed to remove from his flock all what appeared to be damaged and weak for wages. These were the spotted sheep, speckled goat, lamb and cattle. The dominate animals were sheep that were completely white, goats that were completely black, and lambs completely brown.

Laban unbeknownst of God's plan to bless Jacob, jumps at the deal and removes all male and female goats, and lambs that were speckled and spotted. Jacob gave himself a three-day journey, making sure there was separation between his animals and Labans animals.

Jacob counted this as his righteousness and trusted the Lord to increase him. Though the cattle and livestock appeared to be worthless and damaged, Jacob saw beyond what the natural eyes saw and tampered with nature. It is quite interesting that Jacob took fresh rods of poplars and chestnut trees and peeled them back, exposing white streaks on them. He took the streaked rods and placed them in the gutter in the water troughs where the flocks came to drink. The cattle and livestock did drink and conceived. The word conceived here in verses 38 and 39 means that they went into heat so they would reproduce with greater frequency. If you read further you will read what I like to call *Jacobism.* Jacob—a smart man continued to lay the streaked rods in the gutters before the animals that were strong and he increased exceedingly and had many more servants, cattle, camels, and asses. Though Laban deceived him ten times, God suffered him no hurt—Jacob's cattle were stronger.

I was speckled and spotted prey—sequestered by darkness and shame, the world would have called me damaged goods. I was speckled prey that the Lord healed, strengthened, and increased. After a few failed relationships, I found the love of my life out-side of my normal realm—outside of the house, and away from abuse. I married my high school sweet-heart, a man who knew nothing about sexual abuse or what he would have to endure. I dated him in high school and met his family, who loved; they hugged, kissed, and had family gatherings and outings for holidays. Family disputes ended with, "I love you." I had never experienced this. A couple of years later, we married. It didn't take him long to realize that something had happened to me. Though I denied it for years, he knew something wasn't right.

My lack of intimacy caused a pseudo-relation-ship; it couldn't have been genuine until I was healed. I didn't know what love was, so I could not receive love. When it was imparted to me, I rejected it, which caused a strain in the relationship. My men-tal anguish caused psychological pain, distress, and isolation. I guarded my feelings and disconnected myself from people and relationships.

After thoughts of taking my own life, I was ready to give up, so I began to pray. I didn't understand who I was. I was emotionally unstable, and I wanted to know who I would have been if this hadn't happened to me. One day, God sent a messenger; she was someone who had experienced the same abuse, and for the first time, I was able to open up and say what had happened to me. I was also able to share with my husband that I was abused.

Baggage brought into a relationship strains the marriage. Abuse of any kind, if not healed, will be your demise. It affects the roots of the relationship: finance, intimacy, communication, and family. I once heard my pastor's pastor say that a broken woman is insecure; abuse controls the relationship. This is true whether it is with family or friends. It destroys the fibers of the marriage. We will talk about this in more detail.

A Pearl in Process

I was blessed. My husband was God-sent, and he was able to walk me slowly through the process. We were saved together, and God—the greatest counselor ever known—counseled me through the pain. My husband showed me how to love and how to be intimate. He examined the pearl for the first time; he held it in his hand and began to protect and love it. I learned I had nothing to be ashamed of. I was a pearl in process.

The irritations in our lives have the ability to develop us into beautiful pearls. The irritations are the suffering, pain, the grimy freeloaders, the sponges, and the grief. They are also the things we have never discussed. God slowly builds calcium over the grainy, rough surface that irritates the inner shell. The buildup of calcium—God's anointing—produces the pearl. This is not happenstance; we were designed to be gorgeous pearls.

While the pearl is being processed, we are in seed form, hidden from the world and not revealed until the process is complete. What was once a chunk of calcium becomes a perfect pearl. God keeps his precious jewels hidden until the process is completed. Satan thinks he has destroyed you during the cultivation period, but he hasn't. Our pearls cost us something; they are the things we have dealt with. Many of us have had some experiences in life that we chose not to share. If we did share would you judge me or lift me up? We take these experiences to the Lord knowing that He is our vindicator and lifter. These experiences were costly and made us who we are today.

Faith Activates the Completion of the Pearl

If Satan has your pearl, today is the day to take your pearls back. You can walk by faith and demand your pearl.

Faith Pearl Activation Process

Prompted Faith—Hebrew 11:23

"Prompted by faith Moses, after birth, was kept concealed for three months by his parents, because they saw how comely the child was; and they were not overawed *and* terrified by the king's decree" (Exodus 1:22; 2:2, AMP).

Prompted faith allows us the go beyond the natural decree and look to the supernatural power of God to protect the vision and promise of God in our lives and in our children's lives. We are hidden in a secret place with God, where we are blinded to the enemy. God's plan defies Satan's strategic autocracy, allowing us the strength and power to not be moved by what our natural eyes and ears see or hear.

Aroused Faith—Hebrew 11:24

"Aroused by faith, Moses, when he had grown to maturity and became great, refused to be called the son of Pharaoh's daughter" (Exodus 2:10, 15, AMP).

Aroused faith is when you are walking by faith. You serve God and are mature in God. At this point, you no longer accept pharaoh's gifts or presents. You are able to walk away from fornication and adultery. You can get up and walk out of sin—you have taken back your pearls, allowing the only wise God to hold them until the appointed time to release them. You refuse to have any association with pharaoh, no matter what he offers. This pearl is established and will not let the uncircumcised handle it. Your faith has been aroused, and not only are you holding tight to your pearls, but you are ministering to anyone in your path who was sexually abused. You are letting them know that they can also be healed and not feel ashamed. Aroused faith allows you to appreciate the irritation in your life and considers it much greater than the any diamond or ruby.

Motivated Faith—Hebrew 11:27

"Motivated by faith, he left Egypt behind him, being unawed *and* undismayed by the wrath of the king; for he never flinched but held staunchly to his purpose and endured steadfastly as one who gazed on Him Who is invisible " (Exodus 2:15).

Motivated faith will have you walk out of sin and leave a man you can see for Jesus, who you cannot see. Motivated faith will not let you look back, but instead move you toward destiny and the promise. It never complains, but grabs hold of what the invisible God has already given you. My pastor and husband once said, "You begin to articulate praise and estimate worship."

Praise is then coming out of your spirit and not just out of your mouth, because you know that God has an expected end for you. You estimate the measure of your worship. By doing this, anything could happen when you worship—healing, deliverance, etc.

Uniquely Made for Purpose

No two pearls are the same. This is true for humans, as well. We come from different backgrounds and have come down different avenues.

Akoya pearls are familiar—the classic, white pearl—and typically have the highest luster and greatest shine of all cultured pearls. Typical Akoya pearls range from 5 to 11 mm, though the larger are rare finds. The most common and those that are the best value are between 7 and 7.5mm, with a sharp jump in price at anything 8 mm and above. Akoya pearls are either white or cream in body color and typically have a rose, cream, or ivory overtone. Akoya pearls may also be treated to achieve a black body color.

Freshwater pearls can be found in freshwater mussels and are primarily produced by China. Freshwater pearls come in various pastel shades of white, black, pink, peach, lavender, plum, purple, and tangerine, depending on the type of mussel. The typical size of freshwater pearls is 2 to 16 mm, with 7 to 8 being the most common.

We are unique and wonderfully made in Christ. Your pearl magnifies God's glory in your life. This is why God commands us in Matthew 7:6 (AMP), "…do not throw your pearls before hogs, lest they trample upon them with their feet and turn *and* tear you into pieces."

Let's recap. Today, we are not only blessed, but free. It is a part of the pearl activation. It is important to know that you can be blessed but not free, you can even be anointed but not delivered. What am I saying? You can be blessed with a husband, but not free to love and be a wife. You can be blessed to have children, but not free to be the mother who protects, nurtures, loves, and disciplines. You can be blessed with a home, and not free to have peace in the home. The enemy desires to trample and steal your glory—your pearl.

My pearls were stolen until salvation came. Salvation delivered me from the drugs, agony, and nightmares. I was free, and my pearls were in my possession. The pearls' luster was God's glory, being shown in me and through me. I was no longer just blessed, but I was free. I was no longer just anointed but also delivered. I had God's DNA; this also spoke to my personality, my very being. I knew what he intended for me to be—a lustrous pearl.

You can walk as the person God created you to be before the abuse. What does that mean? God can restore you back to your natural state. The fifth healing prescription is yours to accept into your spirit. Know that you have access to your pearls, which cannot be stolen by the enemy. Let us declare who you are today.

Prescription Five

I am a pearl in process that cannot be stolen or imitated—a pearl to which Satan has no rights, a pearl that can only be held by appreciation, a pearl that has luster that never goes dull.

It is the glory of God in me.

FORGIVE AND LET IT GO

The hardest thing to do is to forgive and let go. I am often asked, "Do I have to forgive? How do I forgive?" It is easier said than done. In your most daunting situations, it will take all of Jesus to help you forgive, but to answer your question, yes, you *have* to forgive! Some people have a hard time forgiving during extreme issues. However, I put emphasis on this because I want you to know that no matter how hard it may seem, you can—and must—forgive. In some instances, it is a process. I had to pray with all that was in me to forgive my father—a man who had abused me for years; a man who, when I was grown with my own family, did not acknowledge what he had done. Before salvation, I despised his very presence.

Once God saved me, I read in the Bible that I must forgive. I had to apply the Word. Honestly, I couldn't understand how that was going to happen. I prayed to the Lord and asked him to help me forgive. Even though I said I had forgiven him, I didn't have forgiveness in me. Every time my father came around, something inside of me would rise. I was tense and was full of rage—I wanted a confrontation. This man still had control over my mind, and forgiveness wasn't in me.

When we don't forgive, we are held captive to the situation or person we need to forgive. I later realized that it is just too much power for anyone to have over me. Colossians 3:13 says, "Be gently and forbearing with one another and if one has a difference (a grievance or complaint) against another, readily pardoning each other; even as the Lord has [freely] forgiven you, so must you also [forgive]" (AMP).

Ephesians 4:32 reads, "And become useful *and* helpful *and* kind to one another, tenderhearted, forgiving one another [readily and freely], as God in Christ forgave you" (AMP).

Now for me, this was too deep. God was also commanding me to have a tender heart and be compassionate. Wow! It got deeper as I read more. God was also commanding that I understand and have a loving heart. This is where the struggle was; this is what most of us struggle with.

Let us discuss what forgiveness is. To forgive is to be magnanimous toward the enemy. To forgive and obtain freedom, you must release the person who wronged you to God. You also release the pain, rejection, and hurt to God. To do this, you must let

God know how you feel and ask him to help you release. He already knows, but there is something about releasing it out of your spirit. As I was writing this paragraph, God gave me a vision. I saw a cloud being released; it came up, out of our spirits, and out of our mouths as we released all of our pain to God.

Once you have released this, you can call your abuser's name out daily—even begin to speak well of them. When you first do this, it may sound phony—and it probably is—but keep releasing to God until it is real in your heart. What does this mean? When you see them, hear of them, or think of them, nothing is pricked in your heart. You are then free, and forgiveness has begun. Don't expect this to happen overnight; it takes much prayer and release.

The Redemption

Years later, my husband, family, and I relocated from New York to San Diego, California. We lived there for over seven years. I hadn't spoken to my father in some time, and I got a call one evening. The call was strange; he didn't talk much—just wanted to know how my family was doing. I was curt, as usual, and told him we were just fine. He paused for a moment, then said he wanted to tell me something. I listened. He asked me to forgive him for what he had done. He said that he knew it affected my life. I listened, then told him that he almost destroyed my life.

I knew this was serious, so I stopped and told him I forgave him—that I didn't have a choice but to do so. Later, God ministered to me, *don't get it twisted, you have free will; however, If you love me, forgiveness is in your heart and not just on your lips.* God wanted me to understand that I wasn't doing him any favors by telling my father I had forgiven him. That was the turning point in my life. My father called me to acknowledge what he did. I already knew his time was running short; the Lord had already spoken to me. A few months later, I received a call, informing me that he had a massive heart attack and passed away while having lunch alone at a local diner.

The funeral arrangements were set, and I wasn't sure if I was going to go. My husband spoke to my spirit and advised me that I had work to do, so I went. After the funeral, the family went to my step-sister's house. I was there with sisters and brothers I had never met before; in total, there were five different families represented. These were my father's children. While growing up, my sisters and I were introduced to only one of the other families, with whom we kept in contact. I knew nothing about the other families.

I don't remember how it started, but a woman from each family asked to speak with me privately. They asked me questions about my father. They were upset with my mother and sisters because they felt this man walked out on them to raise another family. He barely kept in contact with them, much less provided for them. Each one of my stepsisters said they were also abused. The difference with them is that he didn't stay long enough to abuse the whole family.

He left the state—traveled north. They knew us, but I did not know who they were until that night.

I knew I was God's ambassador sent to minister to, encourage, and pray for them—to bind up the broken hearts and set the captives free. They all wanted to know how to forgive, if possible. They wanted to know if they would ever forget. That night, they were smeared with deliverance and the healing power. The blood of Jesus is upon them now, and their lives will never be the same.

Is Forgiving Forgetting?

I am also frequently asked, "Is forgiving forgetting?" Forgiveness is not always forgetting. I still remember some things from the past, even though forgiveness has taken place. We have been taught that in order for you to truly forgive someone, you must force yourself not to remember what the person did to you. Forgiveness is not in the forgetting; it is in being free with a spirit of liberty. The grace of God gives us strength to forgive, but this can only be done through Jesus, who forgave us (Luke 23:34, Colossians 1:14).

It is an act of releasing another from an offense—refusing to enact the penalty due to him or her. Forgiving is refusing to let the offense affect the relationship. You move forward as though it never happened. Such forgiveness releases one from a sense of unresolved guilt, restores a clear conscience, and restores a relationship.

To forgive is to grant favor—to show kindness unconditionally. The Greek translation is *charis;* the root word is grace. Forgiveness is a choice to which you commit; you no longer hold the offense against the person.

Though my father has passed away, forgiveness allows me to remember him and his offenses free from anger or grief and with compassion. I now think of a man who was used by the enemy in a most noxious way, who needed deliverance from spiritual wickedness in a high place.

All of the stories told to me about my father's past were abstract. Each story fails to pinpoint time and place. I believe that my father was a victim himself. I cannot imagine what he went through to become what he became, but I do know that he had struggled with this demon since he was a young man, and probably earlier. Just as I ask the question about my offense. I wondered, "Where was his protector?" Satan pounced on innocence and demonized a man who had no clue of the diabolical debacle. This demon came to destroy generations. Today I understand the enemy's assignment. I thought God had left me for a time, but my life was already predestinated. Therefore, I am not mad at the enemy. Actually, I have gained stock in the kingdom of God—experience helps me to minister to others.

You Have to Go to the Next Level

If there is no forgiveness, we cannot go to the next level, and God cannot forgive us of our sins. God cannot go against his own Word.

Matthew 6:16 says, "For if you forgive men their trespasses, your heavenly Father will also forgive your trespasses, But if you do not forgive men their trespasses neither will you Father forgive your trespasses" (NIV).

This is another reason why we forgive; it is one of the most important. Imagine God not forgiving you of your sins and transgressions. Imagine if there was no grace to cover you. We could never make it to heaven. The carnal man would desire us to retaliate against our offenders and take matters in our own hands.

"To me belongeth vengeance, and recompense; their foot shall slide in due time; for the day of their calamity is at hand, and the things that shall come upon them make haste. For the Lord shall judge his people and repent himself for his servants, when he seeth that *their* power is gone, and *there* is non shut up or left. And he shall say, Where *are* their gods, *their* rock in whom they trusted, Which did eat the fat of their sacrifices, *and* drank the wine of their drink offerings? Let them rise up and help you, *and be* your protection. See now that I, *even* I, *am* he, and *there* is no god with me. I kill, and I make alive; I wound, and I heal: neither *is there any* that can deliver out of my hand. For I lift up my hand to heaven and say,

I live forever. If I whet my glittering sword, and mine hand take hold on judgment; I will render vengeance to mine enemies, and will reward them that hate me. I will make mine arrows drunk with blood, and my sword shall devour flesh; *and that* with the blood of the slain and of the captives, from the beginning of revenges upon the enemy. Rejoice, O ye nations, *with* this people; for he will avenge the blood of his servants, and will render vengeance to his adversaries, and will be merciful unto his hand, *and* to his people."

(Deuteronomy 32:35–43 KJV)

God avenges us against our enemies; he takes it personally. Our enemies are his enemies. He reminds them to call on the gods who have led them into the path of darkness. Here, God makes it clear to Israel that there was no other god except himself.

He also tells them to rejoice in the trespasses; God will avenge the blood of his people—you and me. When we are hurt, God is hurt. The Word of God says that we are his great people; we are the apples of his eye (Deuteronomy 32:10; Psalms 17:8). When we are hurt, it is as though the enemy poked God in the eye. The eye is delicate and protected in the socket, reachable for the hands to protect it. God protects the eye.

This is why we forgive and decide to let go, because trespassing without forgiveness does not go unpunished. God can deal with the matter better than we can. David once pleaded with the Lord not to take his Holy Spirit (Psalm 51:11). Though David had sinned, he went before God and asked forgiveness, and God granted him grace. David asked God in prayer to:

- Purge him with hyssop and wash him, that he, is whiter than snow

- Make him to hear joy and gladness that the bones which were broken may rejoice

- Hide his face from sins and blot out iniquities

- Create in him a clean heart and renew a right spirit within him

- Cast him not away from God presences and take not thy Holy Spirit

- Restore unto him the joy of salvation and uphold with thy free spirit

- Deliver him from blood guiltiness

- Open up his lips allowing him to show forth praise

- David also said that his sin and forgiveness allowed him to teach transgressors the way and sinners shall be converted unto God

Once man, no matter what the sin, comes before God to ask for forgiveness, God will forgive. The thief on the cross asked for forgiveness, and God assured him that he would be with Jesus in paradise (Luke 23:39–43). Jesus said, "Verily," meaning absolutely. The thief:

- confessed Jesus as Lord
- asked for mercy and forgiveness of Jesus Christ
- acknowledged justice for crime committed
- acknowledged his own condemnation and helpless state
- feared God, and rebuked another for not fearing God

This gained him forgiveness and access to paradise. Clearly, we must forgive. We do not have rights over anyone, and cannot hold them captive to their offenses. Instead, we must allow God, who knows the heart of man, to judge the situation or offense. This is why Jesus said, "Father, forgive them, for they know not what they do" Luke 23: 34, (AMP).
Jesus, who had no sin, became sin for us. He forgave so that we would be the righteousness of him. Truly, they had no idea what they were doing. The enemy could not stop what took place on Calvary. Jesus is the seed that is still bearing fruit and will until the end of time. Man has no idea. When man offends the people of God, it is best that he repent and ask for forgiveness. This is why you don't have to worry; the matter is already taken care of. I suggest they ask for the blessing upon them, because they have no idea of the power of God.

Genesis 12:3 says that God will bless those who bless you and curse those who curse you. This is a promise, and it is the only place in the Scripture where this statement is found. This was a promise to Abraham.

In Genesis 12:1–3, God declares his plan to beget innumerable children, who will be modeled after the "father of faith." This is confirmed in Romans 4:13, where Abraham's designation as "heir of the world" parallels Jesus' promise that his followers, who humble themselves in faith, shall also be recipients of the "kingdom" and shall "inherit the earth" (Matthew 5:3–5).

We are cursed if we curse others, and God curses those who curse us. Therefore, our prayer is for God to forgive those who have abused us.

Prescription Six

Imbue me, Lord with your anointing, to always forgive. Lord, forgive my enemy, for they know not what they do!

WHAT DOES LOVE HAVE TO DO WITH IT?

Though I never watched many cartoons, I read the comics to escape reality. I never cared for the super-heroes, though. Growing up, I thought the super-heroes were all simulated—sketches of an animated character and far from the truth. I wondered why I should be interested if they were not real enough to rescue me or others like me. My favorite was *Archie Comics*. I couldn't wait to get the next issue to see what was going on in Riverdale. If you are thinking, *They were also caricatures*, yes—you are correct.

Nonetheless, Veronica Lodge was sophisticated and rich. She had no problem with the boys, and her catch was Archie Andrews. She did all she could to scheme and try to buy his love. Betty Cooper was the stereotypical girl next door. Intelligent and of an all-around friendly nature, she was always fighting Veronica for Archie.

I also enjoyed playing with Barbie dolls—dressing them and creating storylines and characters for each doll. My younger sisters had Barbie's whole crew, as well as one Ken doll. When I had my children, Barbie dolls were at a whole other level. Barbie had houses, cars, boats, and bikes, along with other accessories.

The storyline I created during playtime was the relationship I wanted to have when I became an adult. I created a character for each doll. I controlled the beginning and ending of each dialogue, and I created the perfect stories.

When I became an adult, I put the dolls away. However, I always wanted to swap lives with friends, schoolmates—even coworkers. I daydreamed quite often and wished my life were a bad dream. It wasn't until years later that the daydreaming ceased, and I settled for reality. At this point, my exterior was hardened; it was nothing but a defense mechanism. I never had control over my innocence. It was taken away from me. Therefore, I had to be in complete control in every relationship. This is how I protected my feelings and my emotions. I had to keep the guard up. I no longer wanted to be hurt or forced into anything I didn't agree with. I had issues with intimacy, and I didn't want anything to do with close friendships or sexual intimacy with a man or a woman.

Strangely enough, I did marry. Moreover, I shunned intimacy at any cost. For many years, I was in a battle with my mind. I had the mark of slavery, and because I didn't let the past go, I was being mentally raped every day. The enemy, who had given me an ugly and unclean depiction of sexual intimacy and relationships, continued to hold me in a mental prison. It took a lot of prayer to break the curse and stronghold that bound me. My thinking had to change, and my emotional state had to be renewed in God.

The Second Victim

I was in a battle that I thought I couldn't win. I fought off the spirit of suicide. I felt as though I was this strange person—a puzzle piece that never fit. Because of shame, I would pretend to be someone else. As a little girl, I was taught never to talk about the dark past, so I had perfected the art of pretending. I hid my pain and past from everyone I knew, including my husband. I pretended to be a woman who had it all together. Before marriage and in the beginning stages of our marriage, I told my husband I had issues, but I never revealed how deep they were.

My husband calls those around the abused "the second victims." These are love ones who also suffer from the affects. He experienced it and was able to write about it.

Many nights after I was married, I cried and prayed for deliverance for my husband and myself. Though I was a victim, he was the second victim. He was in love with his wife and wanted nothing more than to please her. However, I rejected him. Before marriage, he had no idea of the pain he would endure. His pain ran deep. He battled to encourage and embrace, but he was shut out. Not only was he shut out, but also he was mentally abused. The abuse was from a woman who would seclude herself in a world that refused to let anyone enter. It was a dark place—a dark tunnel leading to despair. The tantrums and emotional outbreaks were enough to make even the craziest person walk away. He experienced a plethora of roller coaster rides. Just when he thought one ride had ended, a new ride began. I was broken, not realizing that hurt and pain prohibits intimacy—they forbid it to enter. My husband knew this, and he prayed hard to save his wife and marriage.

I was the victim, and I made my husband the second victim. I didn't know that I was blessed and fortunate to have a husband who—no matter what I had been through—always remained affectionate and loving. Many marriages could never sustain their vows if plagued with such abuse and a lack of intimacy. Most would have walked out and said it was too much to bear, but because my marriage was founded on love and ordained by God, it withstood what most could not.

When we repeated our vows to each other, we meant them—for better or for worse, in sickness, and in health. That is what we said to each other. Knowing that any one of these could be our portion, we vowed to be with each other until death parted us. That's too deep for the average marriage and for many Christians.

It is typical that we focus on the victims and hardly ever talk about the people who decide to love and embrace the pain of the victims. The second victims are in great pain as well. They often try to figure out how they got into such situations and want to know how to get out of such pain and abuse. When I read Song of Solomon, I am reminded of the love my husband has for me. It is a godly love. This is the love that held the pieces together. He taught me how to embrace love and how to want to be loved. He made intimacy beautiful.

A Godly Love

There is a language of love that echoes and demonstrates openness, growth and a joyous relationship. We have read about the drama in relationships and family: Sarah and Hagar, Leah and Rachel, Abel and Cain, and Esau and Jacob. They were all shaky; this illustrates a need for a new history. If I were preaching, I would say they were crazy.

The Shulamite from Song of Solomon rewrites history. The key word in Song of Solomon is "love." This love presents the passionate desire between a man and a woman. King Solomon, the son of King David, and Bathsheba celebrate with the Shulamite the joyous potential of marriage in light of sworn covenant principals. The Solomonic love personifies love between God and man and applies it properly to both marriage and the covenant history. It exemplifies the ideal wife in an ideal marriage—the covenant people and their history in the Promised Land under the blessings of royal love.

Song of Solomon 2:6 and 8:3 teaches us to freely embrace one another in marriage without rejection, but tenderly and lovingly. Husband and wife must break all barriers in marriage, allowing intimacy to reach its greatest expression. The more intimacy, the more the two become one.

"[I can feel] his left hand under my head and that his right hand embraces me!" (Song of Solomon 2:6, AMP).

The language of love must vibrate in our marriages. What I find interesting is that the church does not want to talk about sexual intimacy when God has given us this beautiful gift. It is legal for a husband and wife to have sex. It is in the plan of God. Two things Christians want are money and sex; however, they don't want to talk about either. Cultivating a devoted marriage helps to heal those who have suffered abuse and need deliverance to enjoy the greatest covenant—marriage. Learning the pure and candid language of love and intimacy helps a couple to eat and drink deeply at the banquet of love. We are then free to allow physical love to nourish marriage.

"He brought me to the banqueting house, and his banner over me was love" (Song of Solomon 2:4, AMP).

"I have come into my garden, my sister, my [promised] bride; I have gathered my myrrh with my balsam and spice [from your sweet words I have gathered the richest perfumes and species]. I have eaten my honeycomb with my honey: I have drunk my wine with my milk; Eat, O friends [feast on, O revelers of the palace; you can never make my lover disloyal to me]! Drink, yes drink abundantly of love, O precious one [for now I know you are mine, irrevocably mine! With his confident words still thrilling her heart, through the lattice she saw her shepherd turn away and disappear into the night]" (Song of Solomon 5:1 AMP).

God's love teaches that the physical desire for a spouse is entirely appropriate. The Song of Solomon is a strong statement of God's covenant of marriage. God knows that sexual intimacy is not to be suppressed. Rather, his intentions are for sexual intimacy within the marriage to be fulfilling, passionate, and exciting. The Song of Solomon covers all aspects. It instructs the newlywed and those who have been married for a half-century.

Joined Together as One

My husband and I have been married for twenty-six years. The last ten have been the best. Every year, I find that we grow closer in all aspects of marriage. A preacher once said about us, "Nothing can come between those two; not even their girls."

This took much prayer and fasting. In prayer and supplication, we joined hands, preventing anything from getting in. God has joined us together as one, healing what was once broken and restoring what was once wounded. It is important that husband and wife grow together and build a godly marriage.

> "Wives, be subject to your own husbands as [a service] to the Lord. For the husband is head of the wife as Christ is the Head of the church, Himself the Savior of [His] body. As the church is subject to Christ, so let wives also be subject in everything to their husbands. Husbands love your wives, even as Christ also loved the Church, and gave himself up for her, So that He might sanctify her, having cleansed her by the washing of water with the Word. That He might present the church to Himself a glorious splendor, without spot or wrinkle, or any such things [that she might be holy and faultless]. Even so, husbands should love their wives as their own bodies. He who loves his own wife loves himself."
>
> (Ephesians 5:22–28, AMP)

Adam was the priest of his home, and Eve was to submit to him. They were the first marriage. Many women cannot comprehend this. *Submit to my husband? I don't think so!* is the response I often get. I am not promoting chauvinism, but this is a command from God. There is an order in the kingdom. Please stay with me; I don't want to lose you. I also had difficulty with any man telling me what to do. I was forced to submit my innocence and my virginity, and I was bitter, but God and his loving kindness came to bring me deliverance and set me free. The Word of God came to bring joy and peace.

Marriage never has to be dull or dead. Conflicts

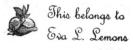

This belongs to
Eva L. Lemons

and misunderstandings may arise regarding sexual availability. However, husband and wife should never deny each other sexual intimacy. They are one, and their bodies belong to each other. Wives should never use sex as a weapon or tool. Intimacy then becomes impure. Our bodies are the temples of the living God, and when we start using them for payment, we are in violation of God's statures. Husband and wife should never separate themselves from each other for long periods of time. This can break communication, and once communication is broken, the natural rhythm in the marriage is broken. This is how the enemy creeps in, and doors are left open. One of my co-workers once said he was abstinent in his marriage. Abstinence should be before marriage—it has no place in a marriage.

> "But he that is married careth for the things that are of the world, how he may please *his* wife. There is a difference *also* between a wife and a virgin. The unmarried woman careth for the things of the Lord, that she may be holy both in body and in spirit; but she that is married careth for the things of the world, how she my please *her* husband."
>
> (1 Corinthians 7:33–34, KJV)

I have talked with many women who have suffered abuse and have a hard time sexually submitting. I share with them that my claim to victory is Jesus. Without the blood of Jesus, I could not submit. After receiving revelation that the man is the protector, provider, and the priest of the home, submission was easy. This is a big responsibility for any man. God has given him a commandment to love his wife. He is responsible to lead the family. To do this, he must stay in relationship with God so he can hear from God, thereby leading the family into posterity. If he is selfish and full of pride, he is held accountable. Revelation of God's plan for the man has kept me on my knees for my husband. I knew my family had to follow him, and I did not want my family to suffer for any reckless decisions.

My responsibility is to help my husband with the assignments he has received from God. I am the help; I came to the marriage already equipped with many gifts. This allows me to be confident, knowing that submission doesn't mean that I am the weaker vessel. I don't need to stand in his shoes; God has given me my own shoes. I don't have to walk in the shadow of anyone—those are worn shoes and a worn pair of shoes has always been uncomfortable for my feet. It is creating something that already is. We are all gifted and our gifts bring us to the forefront as we allow God to use us.

Love is the nucleus of a healthy relationship. Love has everything to do with marriage. Marriage should not be founded on business or a frivolous contract. Jesus is the bridegroom, giving us the purest example of what a groom should represent. He expects us to be ready for the bridegroom and wait with keenness until he comes.

Once the marriage vows have been given, the

husband, wife, and friends will attend a ceremony. The newlyweds walk hand in hand, as they go to the banquet. At this point, the celebration has begun, but it will end the same night if they have married for the wrong reasons—if Christ is not the center of the marriage. After the banquet, they take on life with each other, becoming one—not a business, but a covenant with God. We are to love each other as God loves the church. Salvation teaches and allows us to love like this. Just as Jesus calls us friend, so we become a friend to each other.

Because of love, my husband and I are on one accord. I can actually start a sentence, and many times, he will finish it. Our focus becomes the same; we are equals working in our own realm. He doesn't walk in front of me, but on the side of me. My husband and I work as a team in ministry. Though he is the priest over the house of God, the visionary and senior pastor, I am also the senior pastor, assisting him. I am careful not to usurp the priestly and patriarchal anointing that God has placed on him—we compliment each other. Harmony and communication are the core components of our marriage and ministry. Without communication, the rhythm is broken. To ensure the doors stay closed to the enemy, the love of Christ is allowed to reign in our marriage, thereby making our marriage and ministry whole.

Today, my husband and I teach about the reality of healing a broken marriage. Relationships that have experienced shattered glass due to a relationship collision must release old baggage. My husband

and my family were going on a family vacation. We had just gotten on the road and were driving across the Verrazano Bridge. Unexpectedly, the traffic came to an immediate stop. My husband slammed on the brakes to try to make an urgent stop, but because of the heavy luggage, the car continued to push forward and crashed into the car in front of us.

It is important to understand that there is a penalty for overweight luggage. If your luggage is over the maximum allowance, most airlines will charge you a penalty fee. You will also need to buy gas more often if you are carrying heavy loads in your vehicle. The lesson here is to lose all the baggage. Once that is done, you can move into the healing process. I believe that most marriages can be strengthened and overcome the broken places. What am I saying? I believe and have witnessed that strength is in the broken places. What is broken can be healed and strengthened.

A COMEBACK

A Turn Around

Instead of shame, God has given double honor. The Lord has given a double portion for all that the enemy has stolen. The ruined cities shall be repaired, and instead of confusion, we shall rejoice in our portion. It is a turnaround—what was once desolate is now built up. Isaiah 62 says that we shall be a crown of glory in the hand of the Lord. No longer shall we be termed forsaken, for the Lord delights in us. He has set watchmen on the walls, and they shall never hold their peace, day or night. They are persistently giving God no rest until the Lord establishes us with praise on the earth.

Exodus 22:7 says that if the thief is found out, he has to pay double what he has taken. Satan owes us restitution, and we are here to claim it. Everything concerning our lives is turning around for the best. Every squatter on our property must release it and let it go. We actually have blessings with our names on them; therefore, they must be released to us at the appointed time. We do not accept any substitutes or delays, and we shall not be denied.

Isaiah 45:1–2 gives us an interesting and powerful story about Cyrus who was an instrument used of God to bring the Israelites out of captivity. He devised a plan—a diversion through the water channels, up under the high wall to the two-leaved gate, which was carelessly left open by Belshazzar and the Persian army. It depicts that God goes before us and makes the crooked places straight. He subdues nations and looses the armor of kings to open the double door, so the gates will not be shut. I once had a vision of a long hallway with several doors, and the enemy had someone at each door to block it. Every door held the blessings of the Lord; opportunity, deliverance, and healing. When I walked to one of the doors, the enemy stood tall, hand on hips, and widened his torso to discourage me from going through the door.

He opened his mouth to roar. In the vision, I had to take courage and push past him to walk into my blessing. I learned that we have to take some blessings; the enemy will never freely give them up. He will always try to engage a fight. He knows that most people, including Christians, will not battle for what belongs to them.

Do not be intimidated by the enemy. He has no teeth; he just makes a lot of noise and appears larger than he is. Isaiah 14:16 says that those who see the devil will gaze at him and consider asking, "Is this the man who made the earth tremble—who shook kingdoms?" Those who see will be amazed at what they allowed to keep them captive.

God gave me a strategy for my family. The dream was a revelation about what actually happened. I stopped and asked God for direction. Healing is now coming to my family, and the devil can't do anything about it. God instructed us to have weekly telephone conferences. My family and I came together once a week to rightly divide God's Word, then pray in the spiritual realm, above principalities. As we pray in the spirit, chains that once held my family are being destroyed. The yoke that tied us to Satan is being destroyed. Praise reports are going forth, and the glory of God is being manifested.

God gave me the assignment years ago to war in the spirit. I didn't fully understand it, and at that time, I wasn't prepared to get into anyone's ring. The Lord had to prepare me. I began to search scriptures and read books on spiritual warfare. I learned that God has given every believer authority and power to set the captives free—to heal the brokenhearted and open the prison for those who are bound.

"The spirit of the Lord God is upon me, because the Lord has anointed *and* qualified me to preach the Gospel of good tidings to the meek, the poor, and afflicted; He has sent me to bind up and heal the brokenhearted, to proclaim liberty to the [physical and spiritual] captives and the opening of the prison *and* of the eyes to those who are bound. To proclaim the acceptable year of the Lord and the day of vengeance of our God, to comfort all who mourn, To grant [consolation and joy] to those who mourn in Zion—to give them an ornament of beauty for ashes, the oil of joy instead of mourning, the garment [expressive] of praise instead of heavy, burdened, *and* failing spirit—that they may be called oaks of righteousness, the planting of the Lord, that He may be glorified."

(Isaiah 61:1–3 AMP)

The reference chapter and verse here is Romans 10:15. Those that are called must go and preach to the lost. With experience and the anointing, and the Lord you are equipped to go into the den of iniquity and tell your love ones that God is a healer and they can make it.

Jesus Christ passed this ministry on to his church. The Holy Spirit came down from heaven in all fullness—without measure—to anoint Jesus Christ to set the captive free. This same anointing is in the earth today. Jesus came to bind the brokenhearted—those who are deeply distressed.

I once did a demonstration to illustrate this. I filled a large, tall glass container with water. I then filled a small—water glass with water and placed a few Tic Tac candies in the glass before placing it into the larger container. The large container represents the vessel (you/me), the smaller glass represents the Holy Spirit—water illustrates the degree of the Holy Spirit. It is the spirit without measure within you that is being demonstrated here. While I was preaching, the residue of the candy began to rise to the top of the water. This is what happens when we are filled with the Holy Spirit—the residue of sin begins to rise to the surface. When the water is filled to the brim, it leaves no room for anything to enter. At that point, your cup is ready to run over, and sin cannot enter.

Many people leave this earthly realm in bondage; they do not believe Jesus is who he says he is. They do not believe the same power is here to deliver and set them free. God is a true and honest God. If he said he can heal, he can heal, and if he said he can deliver, he can deliver.

Numbers 23:19 reads, "God is not a man, that he should lie, neither the son of man that he should repent: has he said, and shall he not do it? Or hath he spoken, and shall he not make it good?" (KJV)

I want to clear up any uncertainty by assuring you of his will. It is God's desire to heal all who are sick. This is the will of God. Jesus said that he came to do the will of the Father.

In Mark 1: 40, 41, the leper said, "If you will, you can," and Jesus answered, "I will."

In James 5:14, James asks, "Is any sick among

you?" This includes you if you are sick. Nowhere in the Bible does it say that Jesus questioned the Father to see if it was his will to heal before he laid hands or spoke healing. Actually, Jesus did not pray to the Father for them to be healed; he spoke the healing by commanding it, and they were healed. There was no need for him to ask God to heal them; Jesus walked in the healing anointing.

Jesus did not walk in a spirit of favoritism, for God is no respecter of person. The Word of God says that great multitudes followed him, and he healed them all (Matthew 12:15). It also says the whole multitude sought to touch him, and he healed them (Luke 6:19). We must understand and trust that Jesus is the same yesterday, and today, and forever (Hebrew 13:8).

The same power has been given to you and me. We do not have to question if it is God's desire to heal or deliver. It *is* his will to heal and deliver. We can speak the healing and deliverance over ourselves.

Though it is clear that it is his will that you and I are healed from every sickness, disease, infirmity, and pain, there are a few factors that prevent the deliverance and healing process:

- Uncertainty—not believing it is the will of God

- Disobedience to God and to the Word of God

- Lack of faith—walking in doubt

✧

The author T.L. Osborn wrote, "Healing is God's provision. Wherever faith is taught, faith is always imparted, and the people are always healed." This method never fails, because faith cannot fail.

Exodus 15:26 (KJV) says, "I am the Lord that healeth thee." With positive knowledge of the will of God, we do not ask God if it is his will to heal us or deliver us. We cannot doubt in our hearts, because it cancels faith."

"If ye abide in me, and my word abide in you, ye shall ask what ye will, and it shall be done unto you." (John 15:7 KJV)

When our will aligns with his will, the work is done. Physical and spiritual healing is his will; if we fulfill his promise, healing is ours.

> "If thou will diligently hearken to the voice of the Lord thy God, and wilt do that which is right in his sight, and wilt give ear to his commandments, and keep all his statues, I will put none of these disease upon thee, which I have brought upon the Egyptians–for I *am* the Lord who healeth thee."
>
> (Exodus 15:26 KJV)

How deep is this? If we trust in him, we shall live by faith. Living by his commandments, God will not allow any of these diseases to come upon us.

Jesus proclaimed liberty to those who were captive and opened doors to those who were in prison. He took our infirmities and bore our sicknesses (Matthew 8:17). Jesus came to set free those who were oppressed.

"How God anointed *and* consecrated Jesus of Nazareth with the [Holy] Spirit and with strength *and* ability *and* power; how He went about doing good and, in particular, curing all who were harassed *and* oppressed by the devil, for God was with Him."

(Acts 10:38 AMP)

I like the way Isaiah 53:4 (AMP) puts it "Surely, he has come (carried away) our grief (sicknesses and diseases), and carried our sorrows (pain)"

Jesus came to make us whole. In Mark 6:56, Mark said that as many sick people as touched him were made whole. Both "save" and "made whole" were translated from the Greek word *sozo*.

Isaiah declared, "But he was wounded for our transgressions, he was bruised for our iniquities; the chastisement of our peace was upon him; and with his stripes we are healed." (Isaiah 53:5 KJV)

We have been set free from the prison of our minds—past hurt, pain, and grief. The spirit of heaviness—the spirit of discouragement is replaced by an abundant life, which is the garment of praise. The Hebrew word for garment—*attah*—shows praise as more than a piece of clothing, or just a shawl casually thrown over our shoulders. It unmistakably teaches us to wrap or cover completely, leaving no opening through which hostile elements can penetrate. The garment of praise is the anointing of God that repels the enemy and replaces the heavy spirit. Clothe yourself. Just as we are to put on the believers' armor of God, we are to clothe ourselves with praise.

We have to dress for praise, just like we have to dress for cold weather. Typically, we put on a heavy coat when we go outside; otherwise, we are cold and could get sick.

Praise begins with lifting up the name of Jesus. Please understand the power of worship-filled praise; it has the authority to cast off oppressive works of darkness.

"As many as touched him were made perfectly whole" (Matthew 14:36). God comforts those who mourn. God is the greatest counselor ever known. He gives us beauty for ashes—joy for our mourning, building us up as trees of righteousness.

A Comeback

Claim your healing and deliverance today; stand tall. The ashes have faded away, revealing the beauty of God in you. Have you ever said that it was time to rebound? Well, it is time for a comeback and a turnaround. If you believe the worst is over, then it is. What does this mean? Make no mistake—the enemy will still set up his attacks. There are valley and mountaintop experiences. Therefore, you will not always be on the mountaintop. This simply means that whatever the attack of the enemy, it cannot overtake you.

"But Now [in spite of the past judgments for Israel's sins], thus says the Lord, He who created you, O Jacob, and He who formed you, O Israel: Fear not, for I have redeemed you [ransomed you

by paying a price instead of leaving you captives];
I have called you by your name; you are Mine.
When you pass through the waters, I will be with
you, and through the rivers, they will not over-
whelm you. When you walk through the fire, you
will not be burned or scorched, nor will the flame
kindle upon you."

(Isaiah 43:1–2, AMP)

God is with us. He has given us hinds' feet that
we may walk in high places and stand through the
testing of times. We can acknowledge him in all
of our ways, that he may direct our paths. If we
would allow God to be in our decision-making, we
would not keep turning the same corner, but instead
move toward our destinations. We would then have
choices, and would be able to make the right choice
when it comes to relationships and business transac-
tions. We would see abuse afar away, and it could not
rest in our presence.

"Fear not" is in the Bible 400 times. God wanted
us to know how important is for us not to be fear-
ful in any circumstance. God gives us perfect peace.
Psalms 119:105 and Isaiah 54:17 tell us that God is a
lamp unto our feet and a light for our path, and no
weapon formed against us can prosper. Whatever the
devil tries, it cannot work.

God has turned your life around, and he is the
only one who can do such a thing. Isaiah 55 is an invi-
tation of abundant life. This chapter lets us know that:

- Light is more powerful than darkness

- Truth is stronger than error
- There is more grace in God's heart than sin in men's hearts
- There is more power in the Holy Spirit to convict men of sin than there is power of satanic forces to tempt men
- There is more power in one drop of the blood Jesus shed to cleanse men's hearts from the stain of sin than there is in the accumulated filth of men's sin since Adam and Eve

"For as the rain and snow comes down from the heavens, and return not there again, but water the earth and make it bring forth and sprout, that it may give seed to the sower and bread to the eater, So shall My word be that goes forth out of My mouth; it shall not return to Me void, but shall accomplish that which I please *and* prosper in the thing for which I sent it."

(Isaiah 55:10–11 AMP)

Romans 5:20 reads, "Where sin increased and abounded, grace has surpassed it and increased the more and superabounded" (AMP).

The promises of God have already been established over your life. Let's open our minds and hearts to receive them. Isaiah lets us know that God's Word was spoken into existence, and it cannot return or come back void. The only way we don't receive the blessing is if we don't believe.

We have read about the power and authority that

God has given us, but it really comes down to the power that works within us. We must have the faith of God and become like God in doing so we have relationship with God. The knowledge and wisdom we obtain from God identifies the *degree* of power that must be executed in every situation. When we see our family hurting, when the devil has pulled out all of his weapons on us, what level of power will we use?

Ephesians 3:20 says, "Now to Him Who by the power that is at work within us, is able to do super abundantly, far over *and* above all that we ask or think" (AMP).

We cannot even imagine the supernatural and abundant realm that we can reach through prayer to God. The Scripture does not come to life; it is not activated without action. The fervency of prayer mixed with faith activates the action. This is above our thoughts, desires, hopes, and dreams. There is no limitation in God, according to the promises.

Prescription Seven

I activate the power within me by faith and fervency in prayer concerning my life and my family's lives.

THE MATRIARCHAL CALLING

Eve was the first woman in the Bible. She was the first mother; however, she was not given the promise of being leader over the women. Because of the fall of man, God restructured family and made a covenant with Abraham to make his seed as the dust of the earth. Sarah, the mother of princes, was the first matriarch. She was married to Abraham and lived for 127 years. We can examine her life in three stages:

- *Seven years old:* She was innocent. She was beautiful and youthful. At twenty, she was as though she were seven years old. At one hundred years old, she was as though she were twenty years old. We know this because Genesis 18:9 tells us that the Lord spoke to Abraham and told him that Sarah would have a son. She was then eighty-nine years old. A year later, as prophesied, Isaac was born. The Bible says she was well stricken with age and had already passed the productive age. However, a year after having Isaac, Abraham and Sarah journeyed from north to south. Genesis 20:2 tells us that Abraham told Abimelech the king that Sarah was his sister. He knew his wife was fine and beautiful, and he feared that Abimelech the king would slay him for his wife. This proves that at one hundred years old, she was still beautiful—for all the days of her life.

- *Twenty years old:* Sarah had much strength. Sarah was an idealist. Barren for eighty-seven years, she was a wife to her husband. At twenty years old, she was as sinless as at seven years old. Most people cannot understand the ways of an idealist. Some would say that Sarah was impatient to have another woman lay with her husband to bring forth a child. Others may say it was self-sacrifice that she allowed a beautiful Egyptian princess to become a partner to her husband. Whatever the reasoning, she chose royalty—the aristocrat Hagar, to bear a child. I am sure she pondered on the thought before making the decision. Although it is not clear if she understood the lineage of the unborn child; however, Hagar was probably chosen because she was a disciple of Sarah. In contrast, Hagar was self-satisfied and perceived that because she conceived from Abraham and Sarah couldn't, she was the better. Hagar presumed she would take the role of Abraham's wife, but Sarah's strength was phenomenal. What Hagar didn't realize was that Sarah and Abraham were partners. Sarah asked Abraham to send her away, he listened, and it was approved by God (Genesis 21:12).

- *One hundred years old:* Sarah was full of wisdom. She not only cooked meals for her family and guests, but she was a great leader of the women. She helped to run the family. She was proactive in inspiring and educating the women. Her mantel was passed on to Rebecca, and Abraham's mantel—that of the patriarch—was passed on to Isaac.

The anointing Sarah had on her life—that of the matriarch—should be on every woman. We are called to inspire and educate our families. Ladies, you may have gone through some of the experiences that were mentioned in this book. The devil has come to hinder the plan of God and make us believe that we are insufficient, worthless, or unable to operate as leaders. This is a lie from the devil. Remember Sarah? She could not have children for eighty-seven years. That did not negate the fact that she was to lead the women and be a wife to Abraham. Hagar paraded her pregnancy before Sarah, then tried to take her role as Abraham's wife. This didn't stop Sarah from being the wife God called her to be.

The matriarchal calling is a powerful calling. A matriarch is a tribal leader; her purpose is to save our sisters and daughters from death. They need us. Look around and see how many of our young are lost. We are not the only ones who have traveled this avenue; there are many, and the numbers continue to grow. God teaches us how to live a godly life and prepares us to lead others to his promises of restitution, joy, and healing. The devil doesn't want you or me to make it to heaven. His hope is that you and I hold on to the past, don't forgive, and live a life of bitterness so that our destination becomes one of the cells in hell.

The Place of Preparation

I have come to understand that all I have been through has pushed me into destiny. I lost my sister recently to cancer. I lost my best friend a couple of years ago to cancer as well. With both, I looked into the face of death. I gazed on their lifeless bodies and realized that death has no mercy and is no respecter of person.

The Bible says there is appointed unto men once to die, *Hebrews* 9:27. There is an appointed time for each of us to leave this earthly vessel. Whether God satisfies us with long life or we die prematurely, you will not miss this appointment. It doesn't matter how many tongues you speak; at the appointed time, the

Lord's angels shall come to take you home. If we do not take up the cross and follow him or pursue the calling he has for us, we will go to the pit of hell, where the flames engulf for eternity.

I have walked through the valley of the shadow of death and have discovered that light is in darkness. Multiplication dwells in the valley as well. What am I saying? In tension, there is revelation. Trials reveal that life is precious, and we must do what we are called to do.

Moses, at the beginning of his forty-year wilderness, wrote Psalms 90 and 91. Psalms 90:12 (KJV) reads: "So teach us to number our days, that we may apply our heart unto wisdom." We need the wisdom of God to be successful in whatever we do. Walking through the valley has provoked my tears. My tears, through the pain, have become my healing ointment. This healing ointment is powerful. Though most would like to pray to skip this process, I have embraced it, knowing that you cannot bypass the processes of God.

God alone impresses me and him alone must I impress! He alone makes an impression in my soul. His healing ointment causes you to love everyone. His ointment is able to penetrate and heal all the scar tissue from past pain.

Scarring is common in bodily damage. Medical science teaches us that scar tissue is fibrous connective tissue, which forms a scar. It can be found on any tissue of the body, including skin and internal organs. Because scar tissue has limited blood supply, it is paler and denser than surrounding skin. Though it takes the place of damaged or destroyed tissue, it is limited in function—in movement, circulation, and sensation. Medical doctors can remove scars, but it is most likely that another scar will form after removing the first scar. Most scars do not completely go away. If scar tissue is formed in the heart muscles, it can lead to death.

The ointment to which I am referring doesn't leave any scars—it completely removes them. I have heard Christians say they have battle scars, which limit us in prayer and warfare. This could lead to spiritual death. God is without limits. He can completely heal all scars, thereby making us perfectly healed with His blood flowing through our veins without limitation. Yes, Jesus goes against the laws of medical science and totally and completely heals so that we regain all senses.

The ointment causes you to walk in the anointing of a matriarch. You can love everyone—enemies, sinners, co-workers, neighbors, and loved ones. We cannot lead if we do not love. The healing ointment has caused me to stay in the presence of God. "In the presence of God is provision" (Joshua 1:5–9). I am confident that in the presence of God, the hymen of our hearts can be pierced. Deliverance becomes our portion, making our lives fit for the calling. If the hymen is not pierced, you will remain who you were before salvation.

God is in the valley, and there is victory in the valley. We can look at the Old Testament to illustrate this. With Gideon, the battle was won. It didn't matter that the Midianites were like locusts—great in number. Gideon's men went from 32,000 to 300 men to bring victory. The number three repeats itself here, and the number three means resurrection power. Yes, Gideon and his men were afraid, but God resurrected courage in 300 men. Often, not much is required with God; Moses used what he had—the rod—and the widow borrowed vessels and filled them with the oil she had. The more she filled the vessels, the more the oil was increased to fill all the bottles that were borrowed.

God always wants to prove himself through glorious wonders and miracles. The valley will cause compassion. Sarah had compassion for Hagar, or she would have put her out sooner. Compassion will cause us to love our brothers, neighbors, and those who have spitefully used us. This is all preparation for the matriarchal calling. The matriarchal calling will summon us to rise above the circumstances and know that God is always with us.

My oldest sister is no longer here on earth. God has positioned me to take the mantel—the matriarchal calling for my spiritual daughters and sisters. I have endured much to qualify for this calling. Therefore, the mantel has been tossed to me to lead my sisters. Through prayer and education, I am commissioned to teach women holiness in marriage and motherhood.

A couple of years ago, I was at my overseer's holy convocation when one of my spiritual mothers laid hands on me. She instructed me to tell women what God had said to me. "Give them the truth," she said. The anointing of strength and purity as a mother was transferred to me that night. Since then, I have not been afraid to teach, preach, and counsel God's unadulterated Word.

This book has one purpose—that many lives will be changed and healed. I believe God for the transformation in your life; that you will forgive all and have compassion on all, regardless of what your past may have been. Creation is waiting for us to take our places; we must not look to the past for guidance, but to the Lord. Do not be ashamed, but use the very tool the enemy used to destroy us for the ministry of healing others.

We can make the choice to let go and let God direct us, or we can wallow in pain and complain about the way we are—without joy or hope. I don't believe that God wants us to repeat the cycle of abuse; he would rather we allow him to resurrect us from our pasts. He wants to set us on a sure foundation—a foundation that will not crumble. I am speaking victory!

VICTORY AWAITS

As you were reading this book, what was once dormant may have come alive. Many will have an influx of memories that were once hidden in the corridors of their subconscious minds. A new beginning or lifestyle may also trigger these memories—marriage, newborn baby, etc. This is all normal. You may have had to go back to your inner three-year-old to understand who you are today. People frequently ask, "Where was God in such a traumatic experience?"

Though it may have appeared that the Lord left us for a season, what appeared to be long was only for a mere moment. Seasons are not based on the time of year—summer, winter, spring, or fall. A season could be a week, a month, a year, or several years.

"For our light affliction, which is but for a moment, worketh for us a far more exceeding *and* eternal weight of glory" (2 Corinthians 4:17, KJV).

Rest assured that when the enemy comes in like a flood, God lifts up a standard—making a way of escape and puts the enemy to flight. God comes in like a rushing stream. Isaiah 59:19 discusses struggles with satanic powers. Regardless of what the enemy tries, God knows us individually and knows what each of us can bear. The enemy's attack is strategic and custom-made for each one of us. However, we are stronger than we believe we are. Victory has always awaited us, and God gets the glory. There is an expected end, and it is glorious in him.

You did not just read this book by chance. God has redeemed you and restored you back to your natural state—to the purpose for which he has called you. The enemy thought he had you, but he never did. Sometimes, it doesn't appear that God is moving quickly enough.

Everything that I have been through has strengthened me and taken me from faith to faith and glory to glory. The storm seemed long while I was going through it; however, it was only a mild affliction. It is the storms of life that have trained and prepared me to minister and let many know who they are in God.

We have been set up for the blessing. Lamentations 3:22 lets us know that, because of God's mercy and loving kindness, we were not consumed. His tender compassion did not fail. His mercy is new every morning, and great is his faithfulness. When we woke up this morning, grace and mercy met us. When we put our foot to the floor, it was grace and

EMOTIONALLY WOUNDED SPIRITUALLY STRONG

mercy that covered us. Every day that I can brush my teeth and remember my name is praiseworthy. Every day is a new day—a better and blessed day. We could have been consumed in sin, but because of his mercy, we can let the devil know who we are in him:

- We are a chosen generation (1 Peter 2:9)

- A royal priesthood, a holy nation, a peculiar people (1 Peter 2:9)

- Made in our Father's image (Genesis 5:3)

- He set our feet on a rock and established our goings (Psalms 40:2)

- Redeemed from the curse of the law—from sickness, poverty, and bondage (Galatians 3:13)

- We have overcome the wicked one (1 John 2:13–14)

- Blessed going and coming (Deuteronomy 28: 6)

- The head and not the tail (Deuteronomy 28:13)

- More than a conqueror (Romans 37)

- Above and not beneath (Deuteronomy 28:13)

- I am strong in the Lord (1 Corinthians 4:10)

- I am crucified with Him (Romans 6:6)

- I am seated in heavenly places with Christ Jesus (Ephesians 2:6)

- I am forgiven of all of my sins (1 John 2:12)
- I am an heir to Jesus (Romans 8:17)
- I am an heir according to the promise (Galatians 3:29)
- I am free from condemnation (Romans 8:1)
- I am the elect of God (Colossians 3:12)
- I am saved by grace (Ephesians 2:8)
- I am victorious (1 Corinthians 15:57)

Believe it or not, it is by faith that you are here today. When I didn't know what to do, it was faith that would not allow me to take my life. Religion and false teaching teaches us that faith is based on what you have—the car you drive, the house you live in, the shoes you wear on your feet, or the suit you wear to church. On the contrary, faith is not based on property or belongings. Faith allowed you to finish this book. Faith allowed you to say, *It is me, Lord, who needs deliverance.* Clothes, houses, and cars cannot deliver you from the tormenting affects of the enemy or cast demons and cancer out of your body. Note: This type of religion blocks and prohibits revelation—it is not about religion but about your relationship with God.

We are all given a measure of faith, so we don't have to pray for it (Romans 12:3). We already have it; it just has to be released, and it will increase. Every trial should make us stronger, and every time we come through something, still able to stand, this teaches us that God can do all things but fail.

We have been victorious all of our lives. We were chosen by God before the foundations of the earth. The devil thought he had us but he never did. And because we never knew who we were, we did not know or believe that we could activate the conquering power within us. Though you may have dressed victoriously, perhaps you never lived a victorious life. That was once me. If I was in pain, you never knew it. The greater the pain, the more I covered it with the best outfits, shoes, and accessories.

I still love stylish apparel, but thanks be to God, that it is no longer my mask. This is why women must encourage one another; you have no idea what another woman is going through. If she snaps at you she may be hurting. The attitude is a symptom of what she is experiencing. Yes, she could be dressed to impress; however, she could be torn up inside. Low self-esteem, pain, and tormenting demons cause us to hurt others. But when you have been delivered and experience the love of Jesus; you can only produce his fruit—love, joy, peace, long-suffering, gentleness, goodness, faith, meekness, and temperance.

Eve was victorious and was given everything; however, she allowed the enemy to beguile and strip her of what God had given her. Because God came in the form of Jesus—the living Word in flesh—we were redeemed back to him and given a promise and heavenly blessing. Perfect healing, which is wholeness, was given back to us. We just didn't know who we were in Christ and to whom we belonged.

Victory awaits, simply means that God is waiting for us to come into the full knowledge of who he is—or, more accurately, who we are in him. Once we know who he is, even though we fall, we can be like David who fell with Bathsheba, and the prophet Nathan rightfully confronted him of his sin. Nevertheless, David reminded God that he was born in sin and shaped in iniquity. He identified that, from the time of birth, the propensity to sin is in all of humankind. David asked God to have mercy on him, to cleanse him, and to blot out all of his iniquities (Psalms 51). David took authority over his own spirit, utilizing the power of the Word of God, and restored the relationship between God and him.

Knowing who we are is powerful, but knowing who you are in God is even more powerful. As much of the Bible that we comprehend, that is how powerful we are. Once we believe that we are victorious, the devil doesn't have a chance. The gates of hell cannot prevail against our emotions, finances, family, and health. We literally shut the gateway of the enemy.

To explain this lets' say you purchased a new high-tech computer with many gadgets, components and programs. However, you never learned its full capacity—you never read the pamphlet or instruction guide. Thus, you were limited to what it could actually do.

If we never learn all we can about God—his wisdom, his Word—power, and authenticity, we are limited in the spirit realm and powerless to the enemy.

God Covers All Ground

Let's not mistake the power of God. He is:

- Omnipotent: God is all-powerful (Revelation 19:6). *Nothing* is impossible for him. The only limitation for God is going against his own word.

- Omnipresent: Everywhere, he is present. He can attend to you while he attends to billions of others. He is God—the Father, the Son, and the Holy Spirit—which are all present, where they have dealings.

- Omniscient: God is all-knowing. God gives free will, and he is sovereign; whatever our decision. God is all-knowing.

What is clear here is that nothing goes unnoticed by God. He is powerful enough to shake evil out of its place. As our prayer comes into his hearing, he also listens and responds to other prayers and petitions. No matter where we are, we can call him. No matter what time of day it is, we can call him. We can run into his presence, and we will be safe. He wants nothing but the best for you and me.

I want to make it clear that I don't have to defend who God is—his word speaks for him. God doesn't need anyone to agree with him. He can agree with himself. He is the alpha and the omega—the beginning and the end. He is the great "I am"—Yeshua,

Elohim, El Shaddai, Abba Father. He is the only God who can heal, save, and deliver.

Psalms 35:27 says, "Let the Lord be magnified which hath pleasure in the prosperity of his servants" (KJV). Prosperity means attaining all that is needed to attend to the things of God. It is also God's plan for us to be prosperous and undertake the things of God. This means we are in pursuit of and advancing in the promises of God. We can trust God for his infallible Word.

> "He that dwelleth in the secret place of the most High shall abide under the shadow of the Almighty. I will say of the Lord, *He is* my refuge and my fortress; my God; in him will I trust. Surely he shall deliver thee from the snare of the fowler and from the noisome pestilence. He shall cover thee with his feathers, and under his wings shalt thou trust: his truth *shall be thy* shield and buckler. Thou shalt not be afraid for the terror by night, *nor* for the arrow that flieth by day; *Nor* the pestilence *that* walketh in darkness; *nor* for the destruction that wasteth at noonday. A thousand shall fall at thy side, and they thousand at thy right hand; *but* it shall not come nigh thee. Only with thine eyes shalt thou behold and see the reward of the wicked, Because thou hast made the Lord, *which* is my refuge, even the most High, thy habitation. There shall no evil befall thee, neither shall any plague come nigh thy dwelling. For he shall give his angels charge over thee, to keep thee in all thy ways. They shall bear thee up in *their* hands, lest thou dash thy foot against a stone. Thou shalt tread upon the

lion, and adder: the young lion and the dragon shalt thou trample under feet. Because he hath set his love upon me, therefore will I deliver him: I will set him on high, because he hath known my name. He shall call upon me, and I will answer him, and *will be* with him in trouble; I will deliver him, and honour him. With long life will I satisfy him and show him my salvation."

(Psalms 91 KJV)

This is such a powerful scripture and loaded with promise. Verses three through sixteen are contingent on verses one and two. This Psalm was written to comfort the church in the wilderness through the forty-year curse and to assure children of all ages of God in his providence. The Hebrew word for "dwell" is *yashab,* which means to sit down, to remain, and to settle in the sense of taking up a homestead. The Hebrew word for "secret" is *sether*—a covering or hiding place. Psalm 91 is a promise that if we take up residence in the secret place, God will be:

- A refuge or hiding place
- A fortress or place of protection
- A true and faithful God
- A trust, a place of security

Verses 5–8 mean security for us. We don't have to worry. The destroyer cannot come near us. There is a shield that only allows us to see the reward of the wicked.

Verse five commands another blessing—Satan

and his cohorts cannot overtake us. As long as we reside in the secret place, evil cannot befall us. No disease, infection, curse, epidemic, outbreak, or pestilence can come near us. We are free from sickness; it cannot dwell in our bodies.

There Are Angels All Around

We are well-protected; in obedience and service, angels are given charge over us. The angels accompany and defend us and even preserve us in all of our ways. Our angels are powerful. They operate in the spiritual realms. Angels pulled back the stone from Jesus' tomb (Matthew 28:2). Michael, the archangel, contended with the devil when he disputed about the body of Moses. He did not bring abusive accusation against him but simply rebuked the devil (Jude 9). The angelic realm has holy beings such as angels, ministering angels, archangels, cherubim, and seraphim. There are also demons, as we already discussed.

Ministering angels not only minister to the Lord, but as mentioned in Psalms 91:11–12, they protect and deliver those who belong to him. Let us examine the angels that Psalms 91 depicts:

In 2 Peter 2:8, Peter and his family were protected by angels. In Genesis 19:1–2, 12–17, 29 the angels kept Lot and his family from perishing with the people of Sodom and Gomorrah.

In Exodus 14:19–20, God protected the Israelites from the Egyptians. The angel of God who went before the Israelites moved and went behind them to protect them. It was a cloud that brought darkness to the Egyptians and gave light to the Israelites as they made their way through the sea.

In Daniel 6:22 (AMP), Daniel testified to the power of God, "My God sent the angels and shut the lions' mouths so that they have not hurt me, because I was found innocent *and* blameless before him, also before you, O king, I have done no harm or wrong."

In Acts 5:17–20 and 22–23, the apostles were thrown in jail, and the angel of the Lord opened the prison doors without any assistance from the guards. The guards were not even aware the doors were opened.

In Acts 12, Peter was jailed. An angel woke Peter up from his sleep and told him to rise quickly. The chain fell off of his hands. The angel gave him instructions to gird himself up to his sandals and follow him past two guard posts to the gate that led into the city. Peter thought he was seeing a vision.

In Matthew 26:53, Jesus said he could ask his Father to send twelve legions of angels to deliver him from the Romans, who had come in the night to arrest and crucify him.

Other angels include:

- Michael: Archangel. Supreme commander who does warfare for God—the host of heaven. Name means, "Who is like God." In Daniel, Michael is called "the great prince" who stands guard over the people of God at "the time of the end" (Daniel 10:13, 21, 12:1).

- Gabriel: Archangel. Chief messenger angel. Name means "man of God." He appears four times in the Bible. Gabriel is a trustworthy messenger who brings important messages: the explanation of the seventy weeks (Daniel 9:20–24); the news to Zacharias of the birth of John the Baptist (Luke 1:11–13, 16–19); and to Joseph, whose spirit he settled in order for Joseph to wed Mary (Matthew 1:20).

- Cherubim: Are connected with the presence of God. We discussed these angels in chapter one. Adam and Eve were forced to leave the garden (Genesis 3:24). Lucifer—now Satan—was an anointed cherub who fell from heaven (Revelation 20:2).

- Seraphim: also connected with the presence of God. They are mentioned in Isaiah 6:1–4, where they are described as heavenly creatures. Name means "burning" or "fiery." Cried continuously: "Holy, holy, holy, Lord God Almighty, which was, and is, and is to come!" (Revelation 4:8).

- Angel of the Lord: Scripture refers to these as God's angels, God himself, or the Lord Jesus Christ in what is often called a "pre-incarnated" appearance.

The angels hold us up, lest we go against the statutes of God. Otherwise, we can charge them to battle for us. They can be sent to protect and warn.

Satan, along with other beasts, are under our feet, where his plots and ploys are trampled.

Psalms 91:15 says that when we are in trouble, we can call on him, and he promises he will answer. He concludes with long life—he will satisfy us and show us his salvation. If we believe this is a literal contract that has already been decreed over our lives, there is no loophole in it; therefore, it cannot fail.

Today, we can walk in unshakable, unmovable faith. It is faith mixed with works that perfects our faith (James 2:22). Our heads are lifted because the blood of Jesus heals us. Unquestionably, we are the champion and defeater in every situation.

Sealed with Promise

You were born for the glory of God. Job, who was blameless, afflicted, and given double for his trouble, was born for the glory of God. Lazarus was stricken with sickness, later died and raised from the dead after four days, was born for the glory of God. Regardless of what door was closed or opened, it was for the glory of God. Your light affliction was for the glory of God so that many would know He is the God who can deliver and make free.

> "And the Gentiles shall see thy righteousness, and all kings thy glory: and thy shall be called by a new name, which the mouth of the Lord shall name. Thou shalt be a crown of glory in the hand of the Lord, and a royal diadem in the hand of thy

God. Thou shall no more be termed Forsaken; neither shall thy land any more be termed Desolate, but thou shalt be called Hephzibah, and thy land Beulah; for the Lord delights in thee, and thy land shall be married."

(Isaiah 62:2–4 KJV)

This scripture lets us know that, in him, we have gained a crown of glory and what was once taken—our rightful state in God—can be restored. God is the only God who can bring you back from the wilderness without loss. He is the only God who can bring you into the purpose for which he has called you. Though my innocence was taken in my natural state, in the spirit, the Lord took my hand in marriage. He is my bridegroom. In the spiritual realm, he changes our names, and we are no longer forsaken, but forgiven and we walk with a promise. We are victorious!

Victim No More

Paul, the apostle, contended for the faith that was once given to the saints. He writes in Ephesians 6:12 (AMP), "For we are not wrestling with flesh and blood [contending only with physical opponents], but against the despotisms, against the powers, against [master spirits who are] the world rulers of this present darkness, against the spirit of wickedness in the heavenly (supernatural) sphere."

The oldest trick of the enemy is the philosophy that there is no such thing as a spirit world and the devil is just a figment of our imagination—it is impractical—it is bondage.

The battle is not flesh and blood but in spirit. It begins in our mind. The mind is a battlefield. It is the enemy's playground consisting of thought, perception, memory, emotion, will and consciousness, including cognitive processes to convince despair.

Without the unveiling of the Word of God, the victim remains trapped by a defeatist mindset and is always the victim. There are several meanings to the word victim:

- Suffering, loss, or death
- Tricked, swindled, or taken advantage of
- Harmed or made to suffer from an act
- Harmed or killed by another

We can agree today to change our mindset and replace all doubt. Though we were once tricked—swindled; walking in hopelessness—pretence of a renewed life, we are renewed through Christ. Although we were subconsciously made to suffer the egregious offence over time, we are free in mind and thought through our Lord and Savior Jesus Christ. Hallelujah!

By daily renewing our minds in prayer and Bible scriptures, we comprehend that we are no longer enslaved by the attack of the enemy; we are able to grasp the wisdom of God to know that we are free from chains and bondage. Romans 12:2 (KJV) says, "And be not conformed to this world: but be ye transformed by the renewing of your mind, that ye may prove what is that good, and acceptable, and perfect, will of God."

The unveiling of our heart and eyes allows us to see the ambush of the enemy. When the Word of God is illuminated, it quickens us. We are able to comprehend the depth and height of it; it then penetrates our heart. Subsequently, we shift from unbelief to belief and this is powerful. Faith is increased and we can walk in confidence, absolutely convinced, that we are no longer the victim but the victor.

Webster Dictionary defines *victor* is a person who has defeated the adversary—conqueror. Moreover, Romans 8:37 tells us we are more than a defeater. "Nay, in all these things we are more than conquerors through him that loved us." The Greek word conqueror is *hypernikao*, to gain surpassing victory. We exceed, go beyond triumph and prevail over our adversaries. Romans 8:37 is a promise of conquest and jubilation from God.

Though you may still be in the healing process, God is perfecting that which concerns you. He molds and makes his servants into a purpose driven person. He does not stop until he absolutely accomplishes and completes the work he began, for his purpose in your life.

> "And I am convinced and sure of this very thing, that He who began a good work in you will continue until the day of Jesus Christ [right up to the time of His return], developing [that good work] and perfecting and bringing it to full completion in you."
>
> (Philippians 1:6 AMP)

Isn't this awesome? He ends it with the word "you," he is specifically referring to *you*. You are a good work he started and you are a good work that he will complete. Now that you have come through something like this, you are much stronger. You can stand in the mist of adversity and say that you made it. The enemy thought he had you but you got away. How powerful is that. Congratulations, you are an overcomer!

Keep Moving Forward

God is healing the little child in you. You will never be healed as an adult if the little child is not healed. The healing process has begun. Now, continue to seek deliverance. Remember that you must be delivered and healed before warring for family and friends. Continue to pray—see the prayers that conclude this book. Stay connected to God and it will happen—you will fulfill the promise of God by being his witnessing church.

If you don't have a church, ask God to lead you to a church where the glory of God is evident and signs and wonders are accompanying the Word of God. There must be evidence that souls are being healed and deliverance is taking place. Never stay or get connected where the spirit of the Lord does not dwell.

Now that you have been blessed, pass this book on to someone else who may need to be healed and set free from the bondage of the enemy. Remember—you are spiritually strong—victim no more!

PRAYERS

Prayer of Victory

Lord, I praise you for Psalms ninety-one and I stand on every word. I desire to reside in the secret place of the Most High. Thank you for keeping and protecting me from the snares of the enemy. You are the God who shakes evil out of its place. Lord, you are the lamp unto my feet and light unto my path that directs me in the way that I should go for your name sake. Not my will, but your will be done in my life. Everything that is crooked—things that are not pleasing to you—make straight according to your word and every scripture I have read in this book, hide it in my heart that I sin not against you.

Now that I recognize who the enemy is, I command him to return to me double all that he has stolen. Lord, subdue the nations and loose the armor of the kings to open the double doors giving me clear access to my blessings. Open portals of blessings and make ways for those who are sent to bless me, find me. Remove every obstacle. I accept no delays and no substitutes. I am victorious over the works of the enemy. I am no longer a victim, but a victor. What the enemy meant for evil, God has turned into good. I serve an Ephesians 3:20 God, who is able to do exceedingly and abundantly above all that I ask or think, according to the power that works in me.

Today, I execute and walk in the power of God as I declare that Satan is under my feet. Sickness and disease are far from me. The very plot that the enemy lays for me is returned to him, and I now walk by safely. When the enemy comes in like a flood, my God lifts up a standard—it is a way of escape from my enemies. I have the anointing of David; I speak to every giant situation and command it to come down. I decree that today is his last day, and the Lord will deliver him into my hands. The yoke that was once upon my neck and shoulders has been destroyed. I am strengthened with power. I am more than a conqueror; I am the head and not the tail. I am above and not beneath. I am joint-heirs with you God—a divine position in the Lord. I have been adopted in and now that I also suffer with him, I receive the inheritance. In Jesus' name.

Prayer of Forgiveness

I come boldly to your throne Lord, to obtain mercy and grace in a time of need. I look to the hills from which comes my help; my help comes from the Lord—the Lord who made heaven and earth. Hallowed be thy name; thy Kingdom come today and thy will be done in my life today. God, forgive my trespasses and forgive those who trespass against me. Lead me not into temptation, but deliver me from all evil.

Lord, help me to forgive every offender in my life. I desire to release every offender to you and I no longer hold him or her to the offense. Saturate me with the fruit of the spirit, that I pray mercy for them and show nothing but love and kindness. You are the judge and the revenge. My memories will no longer dictate my emotions. Evil thoughts can no longer control my imagination. I decree self-control. Therefore, I bind every demon that has been sent to control my mind, and I loose the negative effects that have shaped my personality.

I decree that forgiveness will always be a part of my spiritual walk with Christ. For my mind is renewed every day; therefore, I have the mind of Christ. God is building the inner man as the outer man perishes. God I want to see your perspective in every situation that I respond accordingly to the Word of God. I will not judge anyone before their time.

Lord, I acknowledge you in all my ways, that you may direct my path. You have given me power to run through troops and leap over walls. I have the anointing of Caleb, for forgiveness is no longer a giant but it is bread for me. Caleb who was not afraid of the giants in the land, but believed God for the promise and said we can defeat the enemy. He said, *though we are as grasshoppers before them, it is a fixed fight*—the battled is already won. I am blessed of the Lord, in Jesus' name.

Prayer for Our Children

The God of all grace is the protector of our souls. God, you are my strong tower and refuge. In you, I am safe and I can also declare my children and family safe from the traps and snares of the enemy. In you, my children are covered with the blood of Jesus.

Because I walk in the authority that you have given me, I prohibit powers that are designed to cause calamities and violent accidents from being executed. Every plot and motive of the enemy is exposed and dismantled. Every covert scheme is destroyed. My children and love ones are protected from the predator spirit that lurks in the dark.

Bring peace into our homes and harmony between mother and daughter and father and son. Break the yoke that has come to destroy the fibers of the family. Teach us to raise our children in the way that they should go; let them not be another statistic, but successful in you and contributing members of society.

I bind false teaching of doctrines and cults. I

speak to demonic and satanic activity in the airways—TV, mass media, text messages, and e-mails and declare that their schemes and plots shall fail. I declare that by the Spirit of God that the enemy shall be confounded and I loose the effects of the enemy—spiritual wickedness in high places off my children and love ones. I speak to regional demons who have set up residence to influence our young with unnatural affection. Lord, break the stronghold of the enemy off their lives and cause them to be set free from the power of darkness. Break soul ties of unnatural affection—lesbian and homosexual relationships that come to undermine the promise and work of God in my children's life.

Lord, contend with those who contend with us and fight against those who fight against us. Release the intercessor to pray on my behalf, and let them not come down from their watchtowers until their assignments are done. Release Michael the chief archangel to pull out his weapons and have no mercy on the enemy concerning my family and children. You have assured us that if we pray and believe, it shall be done. I settle this prayer in the atmosphere, and pronounce that it is done. In Jesus' name.

Prayer for healing of marriages

Lord, I thank you for your goodness and mercy toward me. You alone are God—King of kings and Lord of lords. You are the God that sits on the circle of the earth. You are holy, and you are righteous.

I come before you today concerning my marriage and other marriages; this was the first institution that was honorable before you. I lift up the broken and torn marriages that healing would overtake them. Bind husband and wife together as one—*Echad*. Seal us in the blood and let no vile, corrupt communication or act enter into my relationships or marriage. The wife is submissive to her husband, and the husband loves his wife as God loves the church. Let each care for and protect one another. Without limitations, cause us to passionately dine at the banquet of love.

Heal the broken wife and broken husband from former abuse. Let love be our portion, that we always exemplify love. Cause the shame to be erased and pain to cease. Oh God, let the intimacy for one another increase to the next level in you, God. I bind every imagination that would come to block the natural affection God has given us for one another and I loose the residue of past pain and torment off our minds.

Lord, cause husband and wife to be free in love and respect for each other. Cause them to hold each other dearly and care for one another; to truly be a friend to one another that they walk this race with character. Heavenly Father teach us to leave a spiritual legacy and a spiritual inheritance. I cancel the plot of the enemy to destroy my marriage. Where it is broken, God you are able to mend and bring it back together as one. Cause husband and wife to seek you for wisdom and understanding concerning the relationship with each other. Every decoy and outside influence that has set up residence to destroy this union I break and dismantle. I declare victory over the works of the enemy.

God move by your spirit in the marriages that divorce would not be the common reaction. But give us endurance, patience, and unconditional love. Hallelujah!

We break the bondage of mismanagement; cause us to be good stewards over what you have given us. We pray that every need in our family is met, that there be no lack. I decree we are wealthy and in good health. We don't borrow, but the blessing of the Lord allows us to lend. I thank you for job opportunities, businesses, promotions, wealth transfers, money to pay off mortgage, down payment for mortgage, all debts paid, all debts demolished, and creative ability without limits in you. Oh God, I love and praise you, in Jesus' Name.

BIBLIOGRAPHY

Floyd Nolden Jones, The Chronology Of The Old Testament, (Published by Master Books 2005)

Maurice Johnson, Destiny Now; Embracing Your God-Given Purpose, (Published by the Word Factory, 2007)

Demonstration of Job, The History of the Afflictions and the Example of Job–page 852, Dakes Bible

T.L. Osborn Healing, *Healing The Sickness*, (Published by Harrison House, Inc, (October 9, 2008)

Herodotus' third logos: Babylonian and Persian affairs - Cryus–Wall of Babylon - *http://www.livius.org/he-hg/herodotus/logos1_03.html* (February 25, 2010)

Hebrew Greek Translation–Strong's Concordance

*http://www.blueletterbible.org/lang/leicon/lexicon.cfm?Strongs=H178&t=*KJV (May28, 2009)

American Baby Magazine, February 2000, p.36 entitled Total Recall/ http://www.essortment.com/all/childrenmemory_rddy.htm (May 28, 2009)

Kinsey Kinsey Institute (Klassen, Williams, & Levitt, 1989),

http://psychology.ucdavis.edu/rainbow/html/facts_
molestation.html (May 28, 2009)

Child Molestation, Ghttp://www.childmolestation
victim.com/statistics.html (May 28, 2009)

Mark Gado, http://www.trutv.com/library/crime/
criminal_mind/psychology/pedophiles/1.html

(May 28, 2009)

Bureau of Justice Statistics: Crime and Victims
Statistics, *http://www.ojp.usdoj.gov/bjs/cvict.htm*
(February 12, 2010)

Census Bureau *http://www.census.gov/index.html*
(February 12, 010)

Child Development - http://en.wikipedia.org/wiki/
Child development (May 28, 2009)

Child Development, http://en.wikipedia.org/
wiki/Human_development_(biology) Human
development, January 2008

Child Development, *http://en.wikipedia.org/wiki/
Developmental_psychology*, Development Psy-
chology, (November 2008)

Citation Guide, *http://www.chicagomanualofstyle.
org/tools_citationguide.html* , (February 2010)

Sexual-Assault Statistics *http://www.fcasv.org/
information/sexual-assault-statistics*, (March 2009)

National Alert Registrar -http://www.registered
offenderslist.org/blog/sex-offenders/child-
molestation-statistics/, (February 2010)

Sexual Abuse - *http://en.wikipedia.org/wiki/Child_sexual_abuse*, (May 2009)

U.S. Department Bureau of Justice Statistics -http://www.unlv.edu/centers/crimestats/pdf/vospats.pdf

Development http://en.wikipedia.org/wiki/Developmentalpsychology (May 28, 2009)

The Diagnostic and Statistical Manual of Manual of Mental Disorders (DMSM III-R)

The National Alter Registrar - U.S. Department of Justice Bureau of Justice Statistics

Laura E. Gibson, Ph.D., University of Vermont, Encyclopedia of Childhood and Adolescent 1998 - *http://www.healthline.com/galecontent/nightmares*, May 2009)

Pearl Guide, Com:http://www.pearl-guide.com/akoya-pearls.shtml (May 28, 2009)

Scar Tissue, http://en.wikipedia.org/wiki/Scar (September 7, 2009)

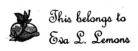
This belongs to
Eva L. Lemons